Understanding
Manna

Daniel James Branagan

ISBN 978-1-64258-452-3 (paperback)
ISBN 978-1-64299-080-5 (hardcover)
ISBN 978-1-64258-453-0 (digital)

Christian Faith Publishing, Inc.
832 Park Avenue
Meadville, PA 16335
www.christianfaithpublishing.com

Two versions of the Bible are utilized in the work. If not noted, the Scripture used is the NIV version; THE HOLY BIBLE, NEW INTERNATIONAL VERSION®, NIV® Copyright © 1973, 1978, 1984, 2011 by Biblica, Inc.® Used by permission. All rights reserved worldwide. Scripture noted as NASB after the verse relates to "Scripture taken from the NEW AMERICAN STANDARD BIBLE(R), Copyright (C) 1960,1962,1963,1968,1971,1972,1973,1975,1977,1995 by The Lockman Foundation. Used by permission."

Printed in the United States of America

Contents

Introduction

"Do you not know? Have you not heard? The Everlasting God, the Lord, the Creator of the ends of the earth does not become weary or tired. His understanding is inscrutable. He gives strength to the weary, and to him who lacks might He increases power. Though youths grow weary and tired, and vigorous young men stumble badly, yet those who wait for the Lord will gain new strength; They will mount up with wings like eagles, they will run and not get tired, they will walk and not become weary." (Isa. 40:28–31, NASB).

This book is about living in an uncertain world and focused on those, who worry about their eternal destiny. Manna was bread from heaven, which sustained physical life during the time when the Israelites wandered for forty years in the desert before entering the Promised Land; however, it signifies so much more. This book is about "bread that comes down from heaven which anyone may eat and not die" (John 6:50). Moreover, it is about *living bread* that "whoever eats this bread will live forever" (John 6:51), and about *living water* that whoever drinks this water "will never thirst" (John 4:14), and "will become in them a spring of water welling up to eternal life" (John 4:14).

Understanding Manna is focused on providing you, the reader, with knowledge and understanding on how to eat the *living bread* and drink the *living water*. Its purpose is to inform and act as a resource so that you can make the most important decision of your life, representing the seminal moment in your existence, and one, which will determine how you spend the rest of your life in eternity. If you do not understand what all of this means, but you don't want to *"work for the food which perishes"* (John 6:27, NASB) but for *"food which endures to eternal life"* (John 6:27, NASB), and if you are yet searching for answers to life's biggest questions, then this book is definitely for you.

Inspiration for this Book

Inspiration for this book originated in 2006, during the time when I was attending a conference in Israel and was severely humbled. Interestingly, the professional talks at the conference went well, as I was very prepared for them, but the failure was not professional but instead a personal one, related to my faith (a far more serious error). The conference was not as well attended due to the heating up of hostilities to the north with Syria and many scientists chose not to make the trip to Haifa. This, however, opened up time for the conference organizers to provide a previously unscheduled tour to the Galilee region. This tour was very exciting, and I was enjoying the scenery from the bus and talking to other scientists, so I missed hearing the announcements from the guide on the itinerary of the trip. I had heard something about the Mount of Beatitudes but didn't think that we were going there because I had thought that it was a high mountain by Jerusalem (smart phones weren't available back then, so a quick check was not possible).

It wasn't long, and we arrived on a high hill overlooking the Sea of Galilee, and as we walked through the grounds of the church, called the Church of the Beatitudes, I realized that this hill was the Mount of Beatitudes. As we gathered in a circle around the guide, she asked, "Are there any Christians in the group?" Instantly, several other scientists pointed directly to me as I had voiced this fact proudly earlier in the week. She then called me forward in front of the group and handed me the microphone and asked me to recite Jesus's most famous sermon. Surprised, I was caught unprepared and was like a deer in the headlights when she stated, "You know the Sermon on the Mount." I had a heart for Scripture for the previous five years and did recall that sermon, and then surmising the situation, quickly deduced that Jesus's sermon must have been here and not Jerusalem. I said that I don't have that sermon memorized, and she pressed further and said, "I thought that you called yourself a Christian?." Internally panicked, I asked if anyone had a Bible (again, no smart phones back then), and she produced one and handed it over.

I must admit further, that in the heat of the moment, I couldn't remember where to find this sermon and started flipping frantically through her small Bible (it was not a study Bible and had no index!). She said frowning, "Of course, you are looking for Matthew Chapter 5!" With this information, I found it, and while flustered, I was able to read the beginning verses of the Sermon on the Mount for the group. The whole incident quite frankly was very embarrassing and certainly I was not a good witness that day. Humbled, I realized that I needed to seriously raise my understanding and improve my Biblical knowledge especially if I was going to openly profess my Christianity. This book, Understanding Manna, is a result of this and written after a dedicated effort of concentrated, mainly independent study, of Scripture over the last twelve years.

Chapter 1

Understanding from a
Scientific Viewpoint

Does believing in a higher power (i.e., a living God) make sense in the modern world? Certainly the viewpoint from the world is no, although if you go to any Biblically based Christian church the answer would be certainly emphatically yes. I can recall an example of this worldly viewpoint from a time spent working in Moldova. While in the car going out to get lunch with one of the Moldovan engineers, I mentioned what a beautiful place God had made. His response was immediate and animated and was something like this, "We do not believe in god and furthermore god has no business in science, god has been relegated to the middle ages." It was said so strongly and as matter of fact, that quite frankly I was stunned as this viewpoint was never my own (but nevertheless and sadly the opinion of many).

Can an expert in a field of science and one trained in the scientific method to analyze and scrutinize data critically and carefully while considering all possible hypotheses before making conclusions, believe in a living God as the Creator of the Universe? As a PhD Metallurgist focused on materials nanotechnology, I would not only say yes but absolutely and unconditionally yes! Observation of the universe clearly shows that the universe exhibits imposed order rather than chaos which signifies design. Design signifies a creator, a rational being who put intricate order and complex structure into the universe and in fact into every length scale which can be studied. Consider the observations of Sir William Blackstone, when he wrote the following, "Law, in its most general and comprehensive sense, signifies a rule of action; and is applied indiscriminately to all kinds of action, whether animate or inanimate, rational or irrational. Thus we say, the laws of motion, of gravitation, of optics, or mechanics, as well as the laws of nature and of nations. And it is that rule of action, which is prescribed by some superior, and which the inferior is bound to obey. Thus when the Supreme Being formed the universe, and created matter out of nothing, he impressed certain principles upon that matter, from which it can never depart, and without which it would cease to be" (Blackstone 1765).

Interestingly, Sir William Blackstone wrote about the nature of matter, even before the discovery of the atom and its make-up was known. Now, we can verify his views of matter, which contains fundamental invariant characteristics as shown for example by the well-known periodic table with each type of atom differing by the number of protons in the nucleus with order described by arrangement of atoms in groups and series depending on their outer shell electrons. Ordered structures of atoms lead to the development of molecules and molecular associations on the angstrom level, which can lead to nanometer level ordering, further replication of order into distinct phases, assemblies of phases to form microstructures (at various length scales), and the formation of distinct metallurgical structures. Understanding and manipulation of this order to reproducibly create structures results in the wide variety of properties we find in materials today which cry out to the beauty and incredible magnificence of the creator.

Understanding Manna is written through a scientifically honed mind, which is in harmony with God's creation. In 2006, after giving two talks focused on materials nanotechnology in Haifa, Israel, to honor the hosts, I concluded by praising the God of Abraham, Isaac, and Israel. After I was through speaking, a German scientist came up and said that he really wanted to talk to me. I thought that this was about my research, and after several attempts, we met on a veranda overlooking the beautiful Mediterranean. He told me that he wanted to speak to me not about nanotechnology but about God. He said his teenage son had recently learned in science class how the universe was made through the Big Bang. His son then asked him, "Who made the universe, was it the Big Bang or was it God during creation, like we learn in church?" The German scientist said that he was afraid to speak out as he was torn by his scientific background and his religious teachings. He could not reconcile these two viewpoints in his mind to provide a proper answer. He also said that this is a very fundamental deep-rooted question and did not want to steer his son wrong so said that he told him that he would get back to him with an answer after his trip. I told him that the answer is quite clear and pointed him to the beginning of Scripture, which states, "In the beginning God created the heavens and the earth" (Gen. 1:1, NASB). Thus, in a singular moment, God created the entire universe from nothing, and time began. The scientific account of the Big Bang involving a singular beginning moment when everything (time and matter) began is simply what we can observe of God's creation—there is no conflict at all.

Another elegant testimony about the concordance between science and biblical teaching was recently provided by Dr. Francis Collins, the director of the Human Genome Project. In a CNN news commentary titled, "Why This Scientist Believes in God," Dr. Collins stated, "I have found there is a wonderful harmony in the complementary truths of science and faith. The God of the Bible is also the God of the genome. God can be found in the cathedral or in the laboratory. By investigating God's majestic and awesome creation, science can actually be a means of worship."

In generations past, it was common for scientists to be believers. Since the development of modern science during the Renaissance Period starting in the fourteenth century, many of the most important and influential scientists were indeed Christians including (a small partial list) Leonardo da Vinci, Johann Kepler, Francis Bacon, Blaise Pascal, Robert Boyle, Isaac Newton, and Michael Faraday (Morris 1990). But what about today's scientists, have their views on God changed? In 2009 in the United States, a poll was done by the Pew Research Center (Leshner 2009), which interviewed 2,500 scientists and 2,000 adult members of the general public. In this poll, 33 percent of scientists said they believed in God, while 18 percent said they believed in a universal spirit or higher power, and another 41 percent identified themselves as not believing in either (i.e., atheists).

These numbers are down significantly from the general public in the same poll where 83 percent said they believe in God, 12 percent said they believe in a universal spirit or higher power, and only 4 percent identified themselves as not believing in either (i.e., atheists). However, this belief in some type of God is not a negligible minority and notwithstanding how the total number of scientists are counted (i.e., scientific degrees vs actively employed in a scientific field), and the associated errors in the survey (+-2.5 percent at a 95 percent confidence level), the poll suggests that there are millions of scientists in the USA believing in God or a higher power.

In 2014, another poll was done by Elaine Ecklund from Rice University and Christopher Scheitle from Saint John's University, and in this poll, they found that 17.1 percent of US Scientists are *evangelical protestants,* which was defined as those Christian scientists stating that "evangelical" describes them "somewhat" or "very well" (Ecklund and Scheitle 2014).

Note that evangelical, as per the Merriam-Webster dictionary, is defined as "of or relating to a Christian sect or group that stresses the authority of the Bible, the importance of believing that Jesus Christ saved you personally from sin or hell, and the preaching of these beliefs to other people." In this same survey, 51.2 percent of *the evangelical protestant scientists* identified themselves as "very religious," 55.6 percent said that they prayed "several times a day," and 85.3 percent when asked what comes closest to your personal beliefs in God identified with the following statement "know God really exists and I have no doubts about it." Based on the results of this survey, it has been estimated that there are over two million evangelical Christian scientists living in the United States (Herman 2014).

While the polls show that there are millions of scientists believing in a higher power and at least two million Christian evangelical scientists, the next question then is whether this subset of scientists represents the second tier (i.e., lesser known or only marginally successful) or would this group be recognized as the top tier of world renowned scientists? To answer this question, consider the Nobel Prize, which is almost universally perceived as one of the greatest measures of scientific achievement. Note that Nobel Prizes are awarded in several different areas including Physics, Chemistry, Physiology/Medicine, Literature, Peace, and Economic Sciences. In 2002, a study of Nobel Prize winners over a one hundred-year period (from 1901 through 2000) revealed that the majority of Nobel Prize winners, specifically 65.4 percent, identified themselves as Christians and another 21.1 percent were from the Jewish faith. Interestingly, only 10.5 percent of total Nobel Prize winners were from the group including Atheists, agonistics, and freethinkers (Shalev 2002, 57). Thus, while the common *wisdom of the world* may be represented by the following statement *of course scientists do not believe in God or creation*, analysis of the works, achievements, and testimonies of scientists in modern times and throughout history, show that this is clearly not the case. Christian scientists, numbering in the millions, have contributed greatly to significant discoveries and advances in all areas of science throughout history, and these contributions continue just as powerfully in the present day as it did in the past.

Chapter 2

Understanding Why This Book
May Not Make Any Sense

As a scientist, I am accustomed to using detailed scientific jargon to explain complex metallurgical mechanisms, structures, and properties in advanced nanomaterials. However, in order to successfully explain these concepts to non-specialized or non-technical people, I have learned to explain complex phenomena in simple terms. Thus, in writing Understanding Manna, I have attempted to utilize easily understood terms and concepts and to purposely avoid complex terms, including Christian terminology, as much as possible, with the goal to write in literal terms and make the information universally understandable, consistent with its original intent. In spite of this effort to simplify, it is possible that this book will not make any sense to you. It may simply be that the information contained within is something that you have never heard before and is foreign to you. If this is the case, as you continue to read and understand each chapter, your understanding may grow quickly. However, you also may find that you gain little to no understanding, even after reading this book once or multiple times. It may even appear to you as written in a foreign language. Furthermore, you may reject the information in this book entirely due to it not making any logical sense to you and may even be disturbed emotionally by the passages of Scripture within.

One might ask then, how can this be as the information in this book about Understanding Manna is intended to not be complex? It is highly unlikely that your lack of understanding (if that is the case) is anything related to your IQ, your intelligence, or your ability to think. The information in this book is often rejected by many of the smartest and most intelligent people on earth (including scientists!) as this is a book focused on godly wisdom and knowledge, which is often a conflicting viewpoint than the teaching, which comes from the world. Thus, the simple reason that you may not understand is that you have been essentially blinded by false teachings of this world and perhaps your own pride. Your situation is not unique as God once called even his chosen people the Jews, "Foolish and senseless people, who have eyes but do not see, who have ears but do not hear" (Jer. 5:21).

Thus, it is possible that *you don't understand because you cannot understand* these teachings focused on Jesus who willingly laying down his life, dying on the cross for all of the sins of mankind, and paying the penalty for your own personal sins. Scripture describes that this understanding "is veiled to those who are perishing, in whose case the god of this world has blinded the minds of the unbelieving so that they might not see the light of the gospel of the glory of Christ, who is the image of God" (2 Cor. 4:3–4, NASB). If you're in this category that the simple message of salvation through Jesus Christ's sacrifice makes no sense, then I pray that your heart is not fully hardened, and that you will read on and continue to seek out truth. Understanding Manna is a guide only to assist you with your journey, as genuine understanding is gained only through the Holy Spirit as

"The person without the Spirit does not accept the things that come from the Spirit of God but considers them foolishness, and cannot understand them because they are discerned only through the Spirit" (1 Cor. 2:14).

Chapter 3

Understanding an
Unchanging Standard

People all over the world and in many difficult cultures share common views on what is considered acceptable behavior and what is unacceptable. Thus it would seem that we are all born with an innate knowledge of good and evil. However, what is the standard of good vs. evil and right vs. wrong? Is it really about your own personal code of ethics? Many people in this world would say that this is entirely the case, that there is no absolute standard. Having no absolute standard means that laws, our societal rights, and even our human rights are a variable and can be given to or taken away at the will of any politician or governmental body. With a standard based solely on the will and whims of mankind, moral decay and societal decline is a probable outcome threatening our very humanity and is a terrifying concept.

An example of this slippery downward slope is what happened in Nazi Germany during the time period of World War 2. To achieve the vision of a *Final Solution* and the establishment of a *master race*, the Nazi's set-up between 1933 and 1945, more than forty thousand labor centers, concentration camps, and killing centers for detention, forced labor, and mass murder including death by asphyxiation using poison gas or by shooting. In addition to untold numbers of beatings, tortures, and rapes, the Nazi regime citing *racial inferiority*, systematically murdered six million Jews, two to three million Soviet prisoners of war, at least two hundred thousand mentally or physically disabled people, along with hundreds of thousands of gypsies, political opponents, and religious protestors.

Thus, history teaches us that without a firm foundation of moral principle, laws can be altered at will and the downward spiral of a society can happen in a relatively short time. After the destruction and capitulation of the Nazi regime, it became clear, from the massive amounts of evidence collected, that the Nazi's had systematically committed mass genocide as well as many other egregious atrocities to mankind. The allied leaders believed strongly that that the Nazi leaders needed to be held personally accountable. However, convicting the Nazi leadership in a court of law through the International Military Tribunals held in Nuremberg from November 1945 to October 1946, proved quite a challenge. The basis of the defense of the Nazi leadership was that they were just following orders from their superiors while obeying the legal laws of the Nazi government and thus committed no crimes. While the separate cases were complex, and the application of international law was not clear, ultimately, many of the former Nazi leaders were indeed found guilty of crimes against humanity, war crimes, waging wars of aggression, and crimes against peace (Wyzanski 1946). The difficulty with the trials was that the prosecutors relied primarily on man-made laws to convict rather than using the concept of *Natural Law*, which was established many centuries earlier by Sir William Blackstone.

Sir William Blackstone was a jurist and judge in England and wrote extensively about the standard of the law in the eighteenth century. Blackstone was most famous for his four-book series, "Commentaries On the Laws of England (1765–1769)", and wrote in Section 2 the following passages related to the foundation of the law, "Upon these two foundations, the law of nature and the law of revelation, depend all human laws; that is to say, no human laws should be suffered to contradict these." With respect to the law of nature, Blackstone defined this as the following, "This will of his maker is called the law of nature. For as God, when he created matter, and endued it with a principle of mobility, established certain rules for the perpetual direction of that motion; so, when he created man, and endued him with freewill to conduct himself in all parts of life, he laid down certain immutable laws of human nature . . ." With respect to divine law, Blackstone wrote that "The doctrines thus delivered we call the revealed or divine law, and they are to be found only in the Holy Scriptures." Blackstone reiterated the supremacy of this absolute standard in the following passage, "This law of nature, being coeval (coexistent) with mankind and dictated by God himself, is of course superior in obligation to any other—It is binding over all the globe in all countries, and at all times; no human laws are of any validity, if contrary to this . . ." Thus, it could be argued that using the concept of *Natural Law* could have been used as a basis for conviction, rather than dancing around this concept during the trials. Notwithstanding the minor role played in the Nuremberg trials, Blackstone's writings had an enormous influence on modern law and it has been stated that in the United States of America "All of our formative documents—the Declaration of Independence, the Constitution, the Federalist Papers, and the seminal decisions of the Supreme Court under John Marshall – were drafted by attorneys steeped in Sir William Blackstone's Commentaries on the Laws of England" (Ferguson 1984, 11).

Laws based on *natural law* and *divine revelation* would certainly provide an unchanging standard of right and wrong. If the Bible is the inspired word of God and if God's supreme wisdom is preserved intact in the Bible, then certainly this Biblical or absolute standard rather than our own malleable personal standard is what we should desire and trust to follow. Through an absolute standard, a firm foundation of moral principles, values, and societal laws can then be established. What does it mean to have a firm foundation? Consider the following parable of the wise and foolish builder taught by Jesus,

> "Everyone who comes to Me and hears My words and acts on them, I will show you whom he is like: he is like a man building a house, who dug deep and laid a foundation on the rock; and when a flood occurred, the torrent burst against that house and could not shake it, because it had

been well built. But the one who has heard and has not acted accordingly, is like a man who built a house on the ground without any foundation; and the torrent burst against it and immediately it collapsed, and the ruin of that house was great" (Luke 6:48–49, NASB).

Thus, having a firm foundation, based on an unchanging absolute standard, can anchor you and allow you to withstand the storms of life which batter all of us.

Chapter 4

Understanding What Is Truth

As was focused on in the previous chapter, basing laws on *natural law* and *divine revelation* represents an absolute standard. This biblical standard represents the mind and the will of God recorded in scripture in the Bible whose words are eloquently described as "flawless like silver purified in a crucible, like gold refined seven times" (Ps. 12:6). Over the centuries, the Bible has been hated by various individuals, groups, governments, and rulers; and many have tried to destroy the Bible and eliminate it from the earth. In spite of these attacks, the Bible remains in its entirety today and is the best-selling book of all time with the second place book not even close. Today, it is estimated that over five billion complete copies of the Bible have been printed in 349 languages with partial copies additionally printed in another 2,123 languages (Guinness Books of Records). Note that these numbers do not reflect the innumerable number of books written about the Bible.

If you have not read the Bible, consider this, that it is the best seller of all best sellers, the #1 most printed book every week of every month of every year. Consider carefully that something inside the Bible must be profound and compelling, since hundreds of millions if not billions of people have read it. Personally, I have diligently studied the Bible for over twenty years (in depth since 2006) and what I have found is that continual study reveals new revelation, fresh understanding, and an inexhaustible supply of new information and insights which are characteristics that I do not find with any other book. Also, I am constantly amazed at how great the knowledge and wisdom is found within its pages. Furthermore, I find that reading the Bible brings forth a strong feeling of inner peace, especially when I am stressed. This peace in Scripture is referred to as the "peace of God which transcends all understanding and one that will guard your hearts and your minds." (Phil. 4:7).

The overriding question is why is the Bible the most printed and best-selling book ever? Notwithstanding all of the items mentioned previously, I believe that this is the case because the Bible represents the living word of God as described in the following passage, "For the word of God is alive and active. Sharper than any double-edged sword, it penetrates even to dividing soul and spirit, joints and marrow; it judges the thoughts and attitudes of the heart" (Heb. 4:12). As an example of how the *word of God is alive and active,* I wanted to relate an experience, which occurred in 2005 as I was traveling to Pearl Harbor for technical meetings. I enjoy listening to Christian sermons on the radio, and while traveling early to the airport, caught part of sermon about a bronze snake statue and how God directed Moses to make a snake and put it on a pole. In my studies up to that point, I had somehow missed this story (or its meaning was yet to be revealed to me), and I was both interested and alarmed since this story seemed anomalous to other ones found in the Bible.

God is a *jealous God* and requires that we only worship him, and it did not make sense to me at that time to direct the ancient Israelites to make a statue since they were surrounded by cultures, which commonly made statues as idols and then worshiped them. In fact, while wandering in the desert previously, the Israelites made a golden calf and were severely punished by both the sword and a plague. Thus, it was very confusing to me that while wandering in that same wilderness, that God would instruct them to make a snake statue and put it on a pole.

This event occurred before the time of smart phones and easy internet access to look up answers but fortunately, I had my Bible with me, and during the long flight to Hawaii was able to find the story of the Bronze Snake in the book of Numbers chapter 21. After reading the story of the Bronze Snake, I was even more confused about its true meaning, which seemed an anomaly in Old Testament Scripture. I became so obsessed on understanding this that I changed my Oahu plans.

It was my first trip to Hawaii and I had a free evening and was planning on exploring before the meetings the next day. However, I both wanted and needed to get to the hotel to continue to search for the meaning of the bronze snake, so after landing, went immediately by rental car to the North Shore hotel. Upon arrival, I had difficulty finding a parking space and circled the parking lots until finally finding an opening. When I got out of the car to open the trunk and get my bag, I noticed that I was parked in spot number 315, which was stenciled on the asphalt. I then looked to my right and saw spot 316 and I thought of immediately, John 3:16, the most famous passage of Scripture. I thought that at the time it was unfortunate that I did not park in that spot. I then immediately checked in to the hotel and went into my room to study Scripture and spent the next hour focused on understanding idolatry, which was no help since God clearly says to not worship manmade idols. I prayed to God to provide an answer, and the number 316 became like a pounding in my head, which I tried to ignore for some time but to no avail.

Finally, I can remember saying out loud, God I know and have memorized John 3:16, so I do not need to turn there. As the number 316 was pounding in my head and would not go away, I finally opened the Bible to read John 3:16. It was as I remembered, so I then started searching Scripture again, but suddenly I stopped and remembered, that I did not park in 316 but in 315. I opened back to the book of John and was blown away that the answer to my prayers was in front of John 3:16 with the particular reference to the Bronze Snake in the sentence before which occurred in verses 14 and 15. John 3:14–15 states, "Just as Moses lifted up the snake in the wilderness, so the Son of Man must be lifted up, that everyone who believes may have eternal life in him." Instantly, I knew the meaning of the bronze snake. The son of Man, who is Jesus, must be lifted up on a pole, which is the cross in order to remove sin for those who believe in order to experience eternal life through his sacrifice (note that the meaning of these verses is described in further detail in chapter 6—Understanding History's Design).

As stated earlier, there can be no doubt about how significant an impact the Bible has made on governments, societies, and individuals throughout history and in the entire world. However, a question, which arises, is whether the Bible is the inerrant truth from God maintained in its original form or whether Scripture has become corrupted over the millennia? If it were like any other book, then certainly the words within would have been changed or corrupted by now. However, the Bible is not like any book and represents the inspired word of God spoken through Prophets who were inspired to write what they were told by God through the Holy Spirit as explained in the following passages,

> "Above all, you must understand that no prophecy of Scripture came about by the prophet's own interpretation of things. For prophecy never had its origin in the human will, but prophets, though human, spoke from God as they were carried along by the Holy Spirit" (2 Pet. 1:20–21).

How did the individual books of the Bible survive intact from their original form over thousands of years? The answer is two-fold and involves understanding how Scripture was copied in the ancient world and also understanding the nature and power of God. Copying lines of Scripture by the ancient scribes was undertaken as very serious business as they believed that they were copying the inspired words of God. Consider the following warning in the last chapter of the last book of the Bible, "To everyone who hears the words of the prophecy of this book: if anyone adds to them, God will add to him the plagues which are written in this book; and if anyone takes away from the words of the book of this prophecy, God will take away his part from the tree of life and from the holy city, which are written in this book" (Rev. 22:18–19, NASB).

Thus, the scribes used incredible diligence during the copying of Scripture. During the time period from 400 BC to 200 AD, the scribes used an organized system of checking Scripture to ensure its perfection by counting, "the verses, words, and letters" of each line and then checking each copied line to the original to know if "there was an error" (Archer 1994, 69).

Without discounting the hard work and diligence of the scribes, consider God, who is so immensely powerfully that he spoke the universe into existence, and who, as described in Scripture, "has measured the waters in the hollow of his hand," who "with the breadth of his hand marked off the heavens," who "held the dust of the earth," and who "weighed the mountains" (Isa. 40:12). Thus, God the Almighty could certainly have kept his word intact in the Bible and in the form and purity, which he has dictated and decided. Additionally, consider carefully the following words of Jesus who said, "For truly I tell you, until heaven and earth disappear, not the smallest letter, not the least stroke of a pen, will by any means disappear from the Law until everything is accomplished" (Matt. 5:18). Jesus thus affirms clearly that Scripture will not be lost including not even the *smallest letter* or not even the *least stroke of a pen*. Who Jesus is and what authority he has to make statements such as this is paramount to Understanding Manna, the focus of this book.

Additional evidence to support that the Bible was inspired by God through the writings of his prophets is biblical prophecy, which was predicted and then fulfilled. A complete study of prophecy is outside the scope of this book. However, it should be noted that Biblical Scripture contains many prophecies with "over one thousand predictive prophecies" and with only "half of these" (LaHaye and Hindson 2006) fulfilled. As an example, consider the book of Isaiah written by the prophet Isaiah around 700 BC. The book of Isaiah contains a lot of future prophecy including predictions related to the fall of Jerusalem and the return of the exiles to Jerusalem. However, Isaiah wrote these prophecies before Jerusalem had fallen and before there were exiles that needed to return.

Consider the following passages from Isaiah,

> "I am the Lord, the Maker of all things,
> who stretches out the heavens, who spreads out
> the earth by myself, who foils the signs of false
> prophets and makes fools of diviners, who over-

throws the learning of the wise and turns it into nonsense, who carries out the words of his servants and fulfills the predictions of his messengers, who says of Jerusalem, 'It shall be inhabited', of the towns of Judah, 'They shall be rebuilt', and of their ruins, 'I will restore them', who says to the watery deep, 'Be dry, and I will dry up your streams', who says of Cyrus, 'He is my shepherd and will accomplish all that I please; he will say of Jerusalem, 'Let it be rebuilt,' and of the temple, 'Let its foundations be laid'" (Isa. 44:24–28).

Note besides predicting the fall of Jerusalem and the entire province of Judah, Isaiah's prophecies even name the king (Cyrus) who in the future would allow the exiles to return in order to reconstruct the wall around Jerusalem, rebuild the destroyed temple, and reestablish Jerusalem as an inhabited city. All of this was prophesized even though Cyrus was not yet born, the Persians were not yet a world power, and Cyrus would not be a king of the Persians, for another 150 years.

Even more importantly, in the book of Isaiah, there are many prophecies about Jesus Christ, which were prophesied about seven hundred years before Christ was born. Consider the following verses from Isaiah, which describe Jesus's birth, life, death, and future kingdom.

Description of Jesus's birth; "Therefore the Lord Himself will give you a sign: Behold, a virgin will be with child and bear a son, and she will call His name Immanuel" (Isa. 7:14, NASB). Note Immanuel means *God with us.*

Description of Jesus's life; "For a child will be born to us, a son will be given to us; And the government will rest on His shoulders; And His name will be called Wonderful Counselor, Mighty God, Eternal Father, Prince of Peace. There will be no end to the increase of His government or of peace, On the throne of David and over his kingdom, To establish it and to uphold it with justice and righteousness From then on and forevermore" (Isa.9:6–7, NASB).

Description of Jesus's death; "he was pierced for our transgressions, he was crushed for our iniquities; the punishment that brought us peace was on him, and by his wounds we are healed. We all, like sheep, have gone astray, each of us has turned to our own way; and the Lord has laid on him the iniquity of us all. He was oppressed and afflicted, yet he did not open his mouth; he was led like a lamb to the slaughter" (Isa. 53:5–7).

Description of Jesus's future kingdom; "Is it not I, the Lord? And there is no other God besides Me, A righteous God and a Savior; There is none except Me. Turn to Me and be saved, all the ends of the earth; For I am God, and there is no other. I have sworn by Myself, The word has gone forth from My mouth in righteousness And will not turn back, That to Me every knee will bow, every tongue will swear allegiance. They will say of Me, Only in the Lord are righteousness and strength" (Isa. 45:21–24, NASB).

Along with the specific verses of Scripture, there are also many additional specific prophecies about Jesus Christ in the book of Isaiah. There is so much prophecy about Jesus Christ that for at least the last thousand years, critics had taught that the early Christians corrupted the book of Isaiah and added specific texts about Jesus. That is, the prophetic Scripture about Jesus, which had been clearly been fulfilled in history by Jesus (see also chapter 5—Understanding the Biblical History of the Universe) was conjectured by disbelievers that they were inserted into the Bible by revisionists after the events in history occurred. While just theories, throughout modern history, there was no way to test these accusations without having a copy of the book of Isaiah, which was written before the birth of Christ so that it could be compared to the modern day version. However, in 1947, a miraculous thing happened to change that with the discovery of the Dead Sea Scrolls in Qumran Israel not far from the Dead Sea. The Dead Sea Scrolls in total consisted of over eight hundred documents including the entire Old Testament (except the book of Ester) with the documents dating from 300 BC to 68 AD (Lawler 2010).

While still debated, it is believed by many scholars that the scrolls were hidden by the Essenes during the Jewish rebellion as the Roman army moved south to Masada after destroying Jerusalem in

70 AD. In these scrolls, there were many fragments of text and also complete books. With respect to the book of Isaiah, not just fragments were found, but also nineteen almost complete copies of the book were found and additionally a complete copy called the Great Isaiah Scroll was discovered. Before this discovery, the oldest known manuscript of Isaiah was from AD 980 while the Great Isaiah Scroll found in Qumran was written more than a thousand years earlier, estimated to have been written from 335 to 122 BC according to carbon dating (Jull et al. 1995, 11–19).

When comparing the Great Isaiah Scroll written at least one hundred years before Jesus was born, it was found that it was "word for word identical with our standard Hebrew Bible in more than 95 percent of the text," and that the "five percent of variation consisted chiefly of obvious slips of the pen and variations in spelling" (Archer 1994, 29). Thus, it was proven that the early Christians had not corrupted the book of Isaiah and the specific prophecies about Christ were indeed written before Jesus Christ was born. In summary, the Bible was written through prophets who were inspired by God through the Holy Spirit and that the original word of God has survived intact to the modern day and has not been corrupted.

Chapter 5

Understanding the Biblical History of the Universe

As described in the previous chapter, the Bible is unlike any other book ever written. In addition to being the inspired work of God, the Bible records the history of the universe from a time before the earth was created to a future time where it will be utterly destroyed. Thus, this book provides an insight of history and the future, which cannot be gained anywhere else. The Bible contains sixty-six books, which are divided into two parts, which are called the Old and New Testaments. The books were written by forty different prophets over a period of 1500 years from 1450 BC to 100 AD. While written by prophets, the Bible represents a collection of inspired works, which are perfectly aligned to tell one story about God's eternal plan. The following sections represent a short overview of the *biblical story* and were chosen in order to provide a basic understanding of specific events and scriptures necessary for Understanding Manna. Additionally, while not even coming close to describing the incredible history, knowledge, and teachings of the Bible, it is hoped that what is highlighted will inspire a future lifetime of fulfilling study.

The Creation

The Bible starts with the story of creation, which highlights the enormous, awesome power of God. God, who exists outside of time and has existed always, spoke the universe into existence. God said, "Let there be light; and there was light" (Gen. 1:3, NASB). The creation of all of the heavens and the entire earth and everything in it occurred over six days. In day one, God created the heavens and the earth and also light. In day two, God created the sky and the atmosphere and created water. In day three, God created land and vegetation. In day four, God created the sun and the moon and the stars. In day five, God created all kinds of fish and birds. In day six, God created all kinds of animals, insects, reptiles, and also mankind. The creation of mankind was distinctly different as "God created man in His own image, in the image of God He created him" (Gen. 1:27, NASB). Thus, God created the first man, named Adam, and later gave him a female helper, named Eve. The world was created without sin or death. Adam and Eve, although they "were both naked," they "were not ashamed" (Gen. 2:25, NASB). On the seventh day, God rested and "blessed the 7th day and made it holy" (Gen. 2:3).

The Fall

The Lord God planted a garden in the East, which was called the Garden of Eden. In this Garden, there were all kinds of trees, which were "pleasing to the sight and good for food; the tree of life also in the midst of the garden, and the tree of the knowledge of good and evil" (Gen. 2:9, NASB). God made one rule that he commanded to Adam, "From any tree of the garden you may eat freely; but from the tree of the knowledge of good and evil you shall not eat, for in the day that you eat from it you will surely die" (Gen. 2:16–17, NASB).

Satan, also called the devil, was made as an angel to serve God, but later became proud of his beauty and splendor and rebelled against God and then was thrown down "from heaven like lightning" (Luke 10:18, NASB). Satan is described in the following passages as one that "does not stand in the truth because there is no truth in him. Whenever he speaks a lie, he speaks from his own nature, for he is a liar and the father of lies" (John 8:44, NASB).

Satan, now disguised as a serpent, entered the Garden of Eden and tempted Eve to eat from the tree of knowledge, which was strictly forbidden by God. Satan said, "Did God really say, You must not eat from any tree in the Garden?" (Gen. 3:1). Furthermore, he told Eve that "you surely will not die!" and that "you will be like God" (Gen. 3:4–5, NASB). Eve then ate of the fruit and then also gave some to her husband, Adam. Through this single act of disobedience, sin entered the world. Both of their eyes were opened and "they knew that they were naked" (Gen. 3:7, NASB) and were ashamed.

Due to their shame, they covered themselves with fig leaves and hid from the Lord God. However, God found them in the Garden and because God had previously commanded to Adam not to eat from the tree, he said to Adam, "Cursed is the ground because of you; In toil you will eat of it All the days of your life. 'Both thorns and thistles it shall grow for you; And you will eat the plants of the field; By the sweat of your face you will eat bread, till you return to the ground, because from it you were taken; for you are dust, and to dust you shall return" (Gen. 3:17–19, NASB). God also said to the serpent "because you have done this, cursed are you" (Gen. 3:14, NASB) and also that Eve's male offspring someday will "crush your head, and you will strike his heel" (Gen. 3:15). God then made Adam and Eve skins from animals to cover their naked bodies and by being clothed with animal skins this act represented the first deaths. Thus, both sin and death entered the world through one man, Adam and the sinful nature of mankind was transferred to everyone who was born from man after Adam.

The Great Flood

Over time the, human race increased greatly in number and become increasingly wicked and corrupt until "the wickedness of man was great on the earth, and that every intent of the thoughts of his heart was only evil continually" (Gen. 6:5, NASB). During this time, Noah lived who "was a righteous man, blameless among the people of his time, and he walked faithfully with God." (Gen. 6:9). God gave to Noah specific instructions on how to make a large ark (a type of boat) made of cypress wood coated with pitch. God told Noah that he would bring "the flood of water upon the earth, to destroy all flesh in which is the breath of life, from under heaven; everything that is on the earth shall perish" (Gen. 6:17, NASB). However, God said that he would save Noah, his wife, his sons, and his son's wives. Noah was to bring with him, two of every kind of living creatures, male and female including birds, animals, and every kind of creature that moves along the ground. Noah did everything as God had instructed and built the ark over many years.

During this time, Noah was greatly harassed and ridiculed. There had never been rain before since the earth was protected by a veil and was humid and watered with dew. Up until the day Noah entered the ark, the people "were eating and drinking, marrying and giving in marriage" (Matt. 24:38, NASB). But at the appointed time, after Noah had done everything as commanded and was safely in the ark with his family and all the animals, then "the fountains of the great deep burst open, and the floodgates of the sky were opened" (Gen. 7:11, NASB) and the earth rapidly flooded. Rain fell for forty days and forty nights, and everything that lived outside of the water was destroyed. The flood continued for an additional 150 days, and after which, the floodwaters starting receding. After a little more than a year in the ark, the land had sufficiently dried out and God told Noah to "Go out of the ark, you and your wife and your sons and your sons' wives with you. Bring out with you every living thing of all flesh that is with you, birds and animals and every creeping thing that creeps on the earth, that they may breed abundantly on the earth, and be fruitful and multiply on the earth" (Gen. 8:16–17, NASB). The Lord vowed that "I will never again destroy every living thing, as I have done. While the earth remains, seedtime and harvest, and cold and heat, and summer and winter, and day and night shall not cease" (Gen. 8:21–22, NASB).

Abraham and His Covenant

The people again multiplied and starting with Moses's son Shem, another ten generations of his line then passed and then Abram was born, who would be later renamed Abraham by God as he would be "the father of many nations" (Gen. 17:5). When Abraham was seventy-five years old he was called by God to leave his country, Ur of the Chaldeans (i.e., modern day Iraq) and go to the land of Canaan (i.e., modern day Israel). According to the tradition of the time, the Lord told Abraham to cut a goat, a heifer, and a ram in half and arrange the halves opposite each other. The Lord told Abraham that "know for certain that your descendants will be strangers in a land that is not theirs, where they will be enslaved and oppressed four hundred years. But I will also judge the nation whom they will serve, and afterward they will come out with many possessions" (Gen. 15:13–14, NASB). The Lord then appeared as a blazing torch and passed through the pieces of animals, thus creating an everlasting covenant with Abraham. Afterward, the Lord said "to your descendants I have given this land, from the river of Egypt as far as the great river, the river Euphrates." (Gen. 15:18, NASB).

Abraham obeyed God and moved to the land of Canaan but he and his wife remained childless. The Lord said, "And I will make you a great nation, and I will bless you, and make your name great; And so you shall be a blessing; And I will bless those who bless you, and the one who curses you I will curse. And in you all the families of the earth will be blessed" (Gen. 12:2–3, NASB). When Abraham was ninety-nine and his wife, Sarah, was ninety, God again declared that he would be "a father of many nations" (Gen. 17:4) and that they would have a son and were to call him Isaac. Furthermore, that "the whole land of Canaan, where you now reside as a foreigner, I will give as an everlasting possession to you and your descendants after you" (Gen. 17:8). When Abraham was one hundred, and Sarah was well beyond normal childbearing age, Isaac was indeed born.

Sometime later, when Isaac was a young man, God said to Abraham, "Take now your son, your only son, whom you love, Isaac, and go to the land of Moriah, and offer him there as a burnt offering on one of the mountains of which I will tell you" (Gen. 22:2, NASB). Abraham, who loved his son, nevertheless obeyed God and did what God said. After arriving at the chosen spot and while making preparations for the sacrifice, Isaac asked his father Abraham where the lamb is for the burnt offering and Abraham replied that "God will provide for Himself the lamb for the burnt offering" (Gen. 22:8,

NASB). Abraham then bound his son Isaac and laid him on the altar and reached out for his knife to kill him. However, God intervened, stopped him, and sent a ram instead, which Abraham sacrificed in Isaac's place. The Lord said that "because you have done this and have not withheld your son, your only son, I will surely bless you and make your descendants as numerous as the stars in the sky and the sand on the seashore" (Gen. 22:16–17).

The Twelve Tribes of Israel

The blessing of God passed from Abraham, to his son Isaac, and then to Isaac's son Jacob. Jacob, who was not the firstborn, had tricked his fraternal twin brother Esau for his birthright and blessing from his father as predicted at his birth that the "the older shall serve the younger" (Gen. 25:23, NASB). Jacob later earned this blessing by wrestling an angel and during this time, Jacob persevered all night even though he was crippled during the fight. God then blessed him, and Jacob's name was changed by God to Israel. Israel later had twelve sons who were Reuben the firstborn, Simeon, Levi, Judah, Zebulun, Issachar, Dan, Gad, Asher, Naphtali, Joseph, and Benjamin. Later on, Joseph's line was broken up into the two half tribes of Ephraim and Manasseh. These sons were to become the twelve tribes of Israel, who would in the future each take a portion of the Promised Land with the exception of Levi, whose ancestors became a tribe of priests and did not receive a territory.

Redemption in Egypt

Israel loved his son, Joseph, more than any of the other sons because he had been born to him in his old age. This partiality caused animosity between Joseph and his brothers. One day, Joseph had a dream that his father, mother, and all his brothers all bowed down to him. When he told his brothers about this dream, they hated him even more. One day, while they were out tending sheep in the wilderness, his brothers decided to kill Joseph. They stripped Joseph of the ornate robe, which his father had given him and threw him into a water cistern, which was empty. While they were deciding what to do with Joseph, Midianite merchants came by, and they decided that instead of killing him that they would sell Joseph into slavery. The traders subsequently sold Joseph to Potiphar, an official of Pharaoh in Egypt. However, the Lord was with Joseph so that he prospered and had success in everything he did. When he refused the advances of Potiphar's wife, she falsely accused him of rape, and Joseph was wrongly thrown into prison.

Even while in prison, Joseph met success and was soon made in charge of all of the prisoners. During this time, through prayer, Joseph was able to interpret the dreams of the cupbearer and baker of Pharaoh who had been put in prison. Two years later, Pharaoh, himself, had a dream about seven cows that were sleek and fat but were then replaced by seven ugly and gaunt cows that ate up the sleek and fat cows. Pharaoh was very troubled by this dream and called all of his magicians to interpret the dream, which they could not. During this time, the cupbearer remembered that Joseph could interpret dreams and Joseph was brought out of prison before Pharaoh. Joseph said that he could not interpret Pharaoh's dream, but "God will give Pharaoh the answer he desires" (Gen. 41:16). Joseph interpreted Pharaoh's dream that there would be seven years of great abundance followed by seven years of very severe famine. The severe famine would deplete all of the resources of the abundant years if careful storing of the provisions during the abundant years was not done and resources carefully managed. Then Pharaoh said to Joseph, "Since God has made all this known to you, there is no one so discerning and wise as you. You shall be in charge of my palace, and all my people are to submit to your orders. Only with respect to the throne will I be greater than you" (Gen. 41:39–40).

The seven years of abundance happened as predicted, and Joseph had storehouses built to store huge quantities of grain. During the seven years of drought, there was great famine in Egypt and in all of the surrounding lands. Joseph, who was governor of the land, sold grain to the people in all the lands from the storehouses. It was during this time Joseph's brothers came to him in Egypt from the land of Canaan to buy grain and all bowed before him as predicted many years earlier in his dream. Joseph tricked his brothers in order to bring all of them to Egypt including Benjamin the youngest. At this time, Joseph revealed his true identify, and his brothers were exceedingly frightened because they had sold him into slavery. However, Joseph forgave them and said, "God sent me before you to preserve for you a remnant in the earth, and to keep you alive by a great deliverance" (Gen. 45:7, NASB). After this, the entire family moved to live in Egypt and settled in the land of Goshen, which was an area with abundant grazing for their flocks.

Removal from Slavery and the Passover

Through the death and succession of several Pharaohs, the Israelites lost their favored position and over time became slaves to the Egyptians and were treated very harshly. In spite of this harsh treatment, the Israelites, while in captivity, became very numerous because they were blessed by God. This alarmed the Egyptians as they were worried that their slaves had become "far too numerous" (Exod. 1:9) for them to control. Pharaoh then issued a decree that every Hebrew boy who is born must be thrown into the Nile to drown. It was during this time that Moses was born from the tribe of Levi. His mother hid him for three months but could not hide him any longer and set him adrift in a papyrus basket. Later, Pharaoh's daughter spied a basket adrift in the reeds and found Moses crying and alone and he became her adopted son.

As he was just a baby and needed to be nursed, Moses's own mother was chosen, unknowingly, by Pharaoh's daughter to nurse him and raise him while young. As a young adult, Moses was brought up in Pharaoh's court with all of the best teaching possible. One day while an adult, he witnessed Hebrew slaves being treated harshly by an Egyptian. He remembered his true heritage having been taught by his mother, and lashed out and killed the Egyptian. He then fled into the wilderness to escape Pharaoh's wrath. He spent forty years in the wilderness of Midian where he also married. During this time, the people that were seeking Moses's death all died, and the "Israelites groaned in their slavery and cried out, and their cry for help because of their slavery went up to God" (Exod. 2:23).

One day while tending sheep, the Angel of the Lord appeared to Moses in the form of a burning bush. God said to Moses I have "seen the misery of my people in Egypt" and "heard them crying out because of their slave drivers" (Exod. 3:7). God told Moses, "Go, I am sending you to Pharaoh to bring my people the Israelites out of Egypt" (Exod. 3:10). Moses asked God who he was and God stated, "I AM WHO I AM. This is what you are to say to the Israelites: I AM has sent me to you" (Exod. 3:14). God also said to tell the Israelites, "The Lord, the God of your fathers—The God of Abraham, the God of Isaac and the God of Jacob—has sent me to you" (Exod. 3:15).

Moses went back to Egypt and he went to Pharaoh and told him that this is what the Lord, the God of Israel says, "Let My people go" (Exod. 5:1, NASB), Pharaoh said, "Who is the Lord that I should obey His voice to let Israel go? I do not know the Lord, and besides, I will not let Israel go" (Exod. 5:2, NASB). Pharaoh was angry and told the slave drivers to no longer supply straw to the Israelites to make bricks but also to not reduce their daily quota of bricks. Thus, the Israelite slaves had to work much harder and their toil was exceedingly great. God told Moses to tell the Israelites that

> "I am the Lord, and I will bring you out from under the burdens of the Egyptians, and I will deliver you from their bondage. I will also redeem you with an outstretched arm and with great judgments. Then I will take you for My people, and I will be your God; and you shall know that I am the Lord your God, who brought you out from under the burdens of the Egyptians. I will bring you to the land which I swore to give to Abraham, Isaac, and Jacob, and I will give it to you for a possession; I am the Lord" (Exod. 6:6–8, NASB).

God, through Moses, then brought on nine successive plagues onto Pharaoh and his kingdom which were the plagues of blood, frogs, gnats, flies, livestock, boils, hail, locusts, and darkness. After each plague, Moses would return to Pharaoh to see if he would let Israel go and each time, Pharaoh, whose heart was hardened, would not let the slaves go. Finally, the tenth plague was to occur, which was the *plague on the firstborn,* whereby all firstborn males in the kingdom "from the firstborn son of Pharaoh, who sits on the throne, to the firstborn son of the female slave" would be killed (Exod. 11:5). God told the Israelites to select an unblemished lamb, "males without defect" (Exod. 12:5) for each household and slaughter the lambs at the twilight of the designated day. Then, they were to "take some of the blood and put it on the sides and tops of the doorframes of the houses" (Exod. 12:7). As explained by God, "The blood will be a sign for you on the houses where you are, and when I see the blood, I will pass over you. No destructive plague will touch you when I strike Egypt" (Exod. 12:13).

At the appointed time, Moses summoned all the elders of Israel and said to them, "Go at once and select the animals for your families and slaughter the Passover lamb" (Exod. 12:21). That night, the death angel was let loose and killed every firstborn male child, including Pharaoh's own son. However, when the death angel came to the Israelite dwellings with the blood of the unblemished lamb covering the doorpost, the house was passed by or passed over (i.e., the Passover) and all the Israelites living in that house were spared from God's wrath. During that very night, Pharaoh summoned Moses and said, "Leave my people, you and the Israelites! Go worship the Lord as you have requested" (Exod. 12:31). The Israelite nation then left, which included "about six hundred thousand men on foot, besides women and children" (Exod. 12:37) "along with flocks and herds, a very large number of livestock" (Exod. 12:38, NASB). The length of time the Israelite people had lived in Egypt was 430 years.

After all of the Israelite slaves left, Pharaoh changed his mind about letting them go saying, "What is this we have done, that we have let Israel go from serving us?" (Exod. 14:5, NASB). Pharaoh took "six hundred select chariots, and all the other chariots of Egypt with officers over all of them" (Exod. 14:7, NASB) and then "the

Egyptians chased after them with all the horses and chariots of Pharaoh, his horsemen and his army" (Exod. 14:9, NASB).

They pursued the Israelites and overtook them as they camped along the shore of the Red Sea. As the army approached, the people were terrified and cried out. Moses answered the people, "Do not fear! Stand by and see the salvation of the Lord which He will accomplish for you today" (Exod. 14:13, NASB). As God had instructed, Moses stretched out his hand over the sea, and the waters were divided and "the Israelites went through the sea on dry ground, with a wall of water on their right and on their left" (Exod. 14:22). The Egyptians pursued the Israelites into the sea, but the Lord threw Pharaoh's army into confusion and jammed the wheels of the chariots. Then the Lord said to Moses, "Stretch out your hand over the sea so that the waters may come back over the Egyptians, over their chariots and their horsemen" (Exod. 14:26, NASB). The water quickly flowed back and covered the chariots and horsemen, and they were all drowned with no survivors.

Manna from Heaven

While initially rejoicing greatly from their deliverance from Pharaoh and praising God, over time the Israelites, while wandering in the desert began to grumble. After 6 weeks of wandering with their resources dwindling, they complained to Moses, "you have brought us out into this desert to starve this entire assembly to death" (Exod. 16:3). Then the Lord said, "Behold, I will rain bread from heaven for you; and the people shall go out and gather a day's portion every day, that I may test them, whether or not they will walk in My instruction. On the sixth day, when they prepare what they bring in, it will be twice as much as they gather daily" (Exod. 16:4–5, NASB). The bread from heaven was called manna and "it was like coriander seed, white, and its taste was like wafers with honey" (Exod. 16:31, NASB). By God's instruction, the Israelites were to gather the manna daily for their needs. If they gathered more than they needed and tried to save some for the next day, the manna would become full of maggots and smell terrible. The exception was on the sixth day where they gathered enough for two days and if kept overnight it would not go rotten. The reason for not gathering/working on the seventh day is the seventh day was commanded by the Lord to be a "day of Sabbath rest, a holy Sabbath to the Lord" (Exod. 16:23). For the next forty years, while the Israelites wandered in the desert, they ate the manna, the daily bread from heaven and it sustained them.

The Law

After three months of wandering, the Israelites came to the Desert of Sinai. God told Moses, who was from the tribe of Levi, "If you will indeed obey My voice and keep My covenant, then you shall be My own possession among all the peoples, for all the earth is Mine; and you shall be to Me a kingdom of priests and a holy nation" (Exod. 19:5–6, NASB). Thus, God affirmed his intent that the Israelites were to be a people set-aside for God. Moses was then called by God to go up to the top of Mount Sinai, and Moses obeyed and went up. At the sound of a very loud trumpet, the "Lord descended upon it in fire; and its smoke ascended like the smoke of a furnace, and the whole mountain quaked violently. When the sound of the trumpet grew louder and louder, Moses spoke and God answered him with thunder" (Exod. 19:18–19, NASB). This scared the Israelites tremendously, and they told Moses, "Speak to us yourself and we will listen; but let not God speak to us, or we will die" (Exod. 20:19, NASB).

God said to Moses, "I have made a covenant with you and with Israel" (Exod. 34:27, NASB), and he gave Moses "the words of the covenant—the Ten Commandments" (Exod. 34:28), which he engraved on two stone tablets. The Ten Commandments from God, from Deuteronomy 5:7–21 (NASB), are listed below:

(1) "You shall have no other gods before Me."
(2) "You shall not make for yourself an idol, or any likeness of what is in heaven above or on the earth beneath or in the water under the earth. You shall not worship them or serve them; for I, the Lord your God, am a jealous God, visit-

ing the iniquity of the fathers on the children, and on the third and the fourth generations of those who hate Me, but showing lovingkindness to thousands, to those who love Me and keep My commandments."

(3) "You shall not take the name of the Lord your God in vain, for the Lord will not leave him unpunished who takes His name in vain."

(4) "Observe the Sabbath day to keep it holy, as the Lord your God commanded you. Six days you shall labor and do all your work, but the seventh day is a Sabbath of the Lord your God; in it you shall not do any work, you or your son or your daughter or your male servant or your female servant or your ox or your donkey or any of your cattle or your sojourner who stays with you, so that your male servant and your female servant may rest as well as you. You shall remember that you were a slave in the land of Egypt, and the Lord your God brought you out of there by a mighty hand and by an outstretched arm; therefore the Lord your God commanded you to observe the Sabbath day."

(5) "Honor your father and your mother, as the Lord your God has commanded you, that your days may be prolonged and that it may go well with you on the land which the Lord your God gives you."

(6) "You shall not murder."

(7) "You shall not commit adultery."

(8) "You shall not steal."

(9) "You shall not bear false witness against your neighbor."

(10) "You shall not covet your neighbor's wife, and you shall not desire your neighbor's house, his field or his male servant or his female servant, his ox or his donkey or anything that belongs to your neighbor."

Moses was with the Lord for forty days and forty nights. and the Lord told Moses "to perform My judgments and keep My statutes, to live in accord with them" (Lev. 18:4, NASB). The statutes laws are often called the Mosaic Law, which includes the Ten

Commandments and additionally moral, domestic, and ritual laws, which were written down by Moses in the Torah (i.e., the first five books of the Bible). The Torah or Law set up a standard of holiness for a people who are to be set apart and also as a witness and standard for all other nations.

Establishment of Sacrifice for Atonement of Sins

As part of the Law provided to the Israelites, a system was established for ceremonial sacrifice to honor the Lord. The Lord said to Moses to "construct a sanctuary for Me, that I may dwell among them" (Exod. 25:8, NASB). The Lord provided very specific and detailed instructions on how this sanctuary was to be built. The Tent of Meeting consisted of sixty wooden pillars with fine linen curtains, which contained an area like a courtyard. Inside the courtyard was the Tabernacle, which was a type of tent, and which enclosed the Holy Place and the Holy of Holies. The Israelites could enter the courtyard, but only the Levitical priests could enter the Tabernacle. Between the courtyard and the Holy Place and the Most Holy Place, there were veils, which separated each area.

In the Holy Place, the Levitical Priests performed ritual rites to honor God and to pray for the sins of the people. In the Holy of Holies, the Ark of the Covenant was placed and this area was reserved for God to dwell in his presence. Once a year, the high priest on the Day of Atonement would "slaughter the goat of the sin offering which is for the people, and bring its blood inside the veil" (Lev. 16:15, NASB). Then the high priest would enter the Holy of Holies where he would "sprinkle it" (Lev. 16:15, NASB) and "make atonement for the Most Holy Place because of the uncleanness and rebellion of the Israelites, whatever their sins have been" (Lev. 16:16). Thus, by this process, the high priest was able to intercede for the sins of the Israelite people individually and as a nation. The ceremony had to be repeated each and every year at the appointed time since the blood of the animals did not remove sin, but instead was only able to atone/cover the sins of the Israelites.

After the Tent of Meeting was constructed, a "cloud covered the tent of meeting, and the glory of the Lord filled the tabernacle" (Exod. 40:34, NASB). Whenever the cloud lifted from above the tabernacle, the Israelites would set out and if it did not lift, they did not set out and "throughout all their journeys, the cloud of the Lord was on the tabernacle by day, and there was fire in it by night, in the sight of all the house of Israel" (Exod. 40:38, NASB). By the guidance of the Lord, the Israelites' path was directed for the forty years spent in the wilderness.

The Golden Calf

During this time of wandering in the wilderness, Moses went up one day on a mountain to speak directly to God and spoke with God for a long time. The Israelites became restless and so gathered up their gold earrings and jewelry, melted them, and cast the liquid into a golden calf. Then, the people committed blasphemy by saying, "These are your gods, Israel, who brought you up out of Egypt" and starting worshiping it as an idol and "built an altar before it" (Exod. 32:4–5, NASB). God saw all of this, was very angry, and sent Moses back to the people. When Moses returned, he was very upset for their worshiping of the false idol instead of the living God. Moses destroyed the golden calf, and he ordered the Levites to punish the people and three thousand died by the sword. Because of their sin of idolatry, the punishment from God was also very severe, and many more perished later from a plague sent by the Lord.

The Bronze Snake

At a later time, the Israelites again became disobedient and "spoke against God and against Moses, and said, "Why have you brought us up out of Egypt to die in the wilderness? There is no bread! There is no water! And we detest this miserable food!" (Num. 21:5). To punish them, God sent in poisonous snakes, and many of the Israelites were bitten and died. The people realizing that they had sinned against God, repented of their sins. God then instructed

Moses to "make a snake and put it up on a pole; anyone who is bitten can look at it and live" (Num. 21:8). Thus, once anyone was bitten by a poisonous snake, they went to the bronze snake, looked upon it, and were healed.

The Promised Land

After wandering in the desert for forty years, the Israelites were brought to the boundary of the Promised Land. The Lord said to Moses, "Send some men to explore the land of Canaan, which I am giving to the Israelites. From each ancestral tribe send one of its leaders" (Num. 13:2). Moses then sent the spies into the land of Canaan, and they explored the land for forty days. The spies then returned and gave the following report to all of the Israelites, "We went in to the land where you sent us; and it certainly does flow with milk and honey, and this is its fruit. Nevertheless, the people who live in the land are strong, and the cities are fortified and very large" (Num. 13:27–28, NASB). Then Caleb, one of the spies, silenced the people before Moses and said, "We should by all means go up and take possession of it, for we will surely overcome it" (Num. 13:30, NASB). But the men who had gone up with him said, "We can't attack those people; they are stronger than we are. And they spread among the Israelites a bad report about the land they had explored" (Num. 13:31–32).

Even though God told them to go enter the Promised Land, the Israelites did not trust God, were afraid of the people and their fortifications, and did not enter. In punishment, God said "In this wilderness your bodies will fall—every one of you twenty years old or more who was counted in the census and who has grumbled against me. Not one of you will enter the land I swore with uplifted hand to make your home, except Caleb son of Jephunneh and Joshua son of Nun. As for your children that you said would be taken as plunder, I will bring them in to enjoy the land you have rejected. But as for you, your bodies will fall in this wilderness" (Num. 14:29–32).

Forty years later, after the previous generation all passed away including their leader, Moses; Joshua, who succeeded Moses as leader, led the Israelites into Canaan. The Israelites' first victory occurred when they captured the city of Jericho bringing down the heavily fortified wall by obeying God's specific instructions. After circling the city seven times, "priests blew the trumpets; and when the people heard the sound of the trumpet, the people shouted with a great shout and the wall fell down flat, so that the people went up into the city, every man straight ahead, and they took the city" (Josh. 6:20, NASB). After capturing Jericho, the Israelites won a series of battles against their surrounding nations in rapid succession and began to establish themselves in the Promised Land, which was flowing with milk and honey.

The Time of the Judges

After the Israelites entered the Promised Land, they continued to conquer territory and eventually became a great nation. The nation of Israel was unique among all of the nations of the world as they were "a holy people to the Lord," which the Lord had chosen "to be a people for His own possession out of all the peoples who are on the face of the earth" (Deut. 7:6, NASB). As an example of God's strong belief in justice, he told the Israelites to set up six cities of refuge, which were placed in strategic locations on either side of the Jordan River. These cities of refuge were places of sanctuary where "a person who has killed someone accidentally may flee" (Num. 35:11), and then could reside in safety until they stood trial "before the assembly." (Num. 35:12).

Unlike other nations, the Israelites did not have a king, as God was their true King, but instead relied on Judges, who were both prophets and leaders. Judges administered to the Israelites in many ways including militarily and spiritually, judged disputes, interpreted laws, and provided leadership during times of crisis. Over 350 years, God rose up fifteen different Judges to address the challenges facing the people as their needs arose. During this entire period, there was a general recurring pattern of rebellion and idolatry and then punishment by the Lord, followed by a time of repentance and cleansing with the removal of idols from the land, and worshiping of the only true God. The Lord's punishment during rebellion was often in the form of invasion by enemy nations, and during this time, the Israelites were invaded by, and had war with, many nations including the Moabites, Ammonites, Canaanites, Amalekites, Midianites, and Philistines.

The story of Gideon is representative of how God raised up Judges during this time period. In 1150 BC, the Israelites "did what was evil in the sight of the Lord; and the Lord gave them into the hands of Midian seven years" (Judg. 6:1, NASB). The power of Midian was so oppressive that the Israelites "prepared shelters for themselves in mountain clefts, caves and strongholds" (Judg. 6:2), the invaders "ruined the crops," and "did not spare a living thing for Israel" (Judg. 6:4).

Through successive invasions over a period of seven years, the Midianites "so impoverished the Israelites that they cried out to the Lord for help" (Judg. 6:6). Then, the angel of the Lord appeared to Gideon, and said, "The Lord is with you, mighty warrior." Gideon replied, "if the Lord is with us, why has all this happened to us?." The Lord turned to him and said, "Go in this your strength and deliver Israel from the hand of Midian. Have I not sent you?" (Judg. 6:12-14, NASB).

Gideon replied, "Lord, how shall I deliver Israel? Behold, my family is the least in Manasseh, and I am the youngest in my father's house." The Lord answered, "Surely I will be with you" (Judg. 6:15–16, NASB). Gideon, after preparing an offering to the Lord, took ten men and tore down the foreign idols, which included altars to Baal and the Asherah poles. These acts were reported and roused the anger of Israel's enemies, including the Midianites and Amalekites, as they worshiped these false idols and they joined forces to destroy the Israelites. Faced with almost certain destruction, Gideon tested the Lord and received clear signs that the Lord was behind him and that he was chosen by God to become a great leader.

Gideon sent messengers throughout the land asking for help and thirty-two thousand men came forward from the tribes of Manasseh, Asher, Zebulun and Naphtali to defend Israel. However, the Lord said to Gideon, "You have too many men," and when the Midianites are defeated the Israelites would boast that their "own strength has saved" them (Judg. 7:2). The Lord told Gideon to announce that "whoever is afraid and trembling, let him return and depart" and with the announcement "twenty-two thousand men left, while ten thousand remained" (Judg. 7:3). Next, the Lord said to Gideon, "There are still too many men. Take them down to the water, and I will thin them out for you there" (Judg. 7:4). Gideon took the men down to the water and the Lord told him, "You shall separate everyone who laps the water with his tongue as a dog laps, as well as everyone who kneels to drink" (Judg. 7:5, NASB).

Three hundred of them drank from cupped hands, lapping like dogs, and the Lord said to Gideon, "I will deliver you with the 300 men who lapped and will give the Midianites into your hands; so let all the other people go" (Judg. 7:7, NSAB). Gideon then sent the rest of the Israelites home except the chosen three hundred.

During that night, the Lord said to Gideon, "Arise, go down against the camp, for I have given it into your hands" (Judg. 7:9, NASB). Gideon and his men went to the enemy's camp and divided into three groups. Following God's instructions, they blew their trumpets and broke the jars that were in their hands and they shouted, "A sword for the Lord and for Gideon!" (Judg. 7:20, NASB). The large army of the Midianites, who had been tormented by dreams about their destruction by the Israelites, then panicked and fled. They were pursued by the Israelites and driven out of the hill country to the Jordan River and their leaders were killed.

Afterward, the Israelites said to Gideon, "Rule over us, both you and your son, also your son's son, for you have delivered us from the hand of Midian" (Judg. 8:22, NASB). But Gideon told them, "I will not rule over you, nor shall my son rule over you; the Lord shall rule over you" (Judg. 8:23, NASB). For the next forty years with Gideon as their leader, the Israelites had peace from their enemies. However, when Gideon died, the "Israelites again prostituted themselves to the Baal's and returned to their idolatry" (Judg. 8:33). Nevertheless, Gideon, like the other Judges who were raised up by the Lord,

"by faith conquered kingdoms, performed
acts of righteousness, obtained promises, shut

the mouths of lions, quenched the power of fire, escaped the edge of the sword, from weakness were made strong, became mighty in war, put foreign armies to flight" (Heb. 11:33–34, NASB).

The Time of the Kings

During one period of rebellion, the Israelites demanded that they have a king like all of the other nations. The people went to Samuel, who was to be the last judge, and said to him "Give us a king to lead us" (1 Sam. 8:6). Samuel was displeased by their demands and prayed to the Lord. The Lord said, "Listen to the voice of the people in regard to all that they say to you, for they have not rejected you, but they have rejected Me from being king over them" (1 Sam. 8:7, NASB). The Lord also said, "But warn them solemnly and let them know what the king who will reign over them will claim as his rights" (1 Sam. 8:9).

Samuel then gave the Lord's warning to the people that the King will take

"your sons and place them for himself in his chariots and among his horsemen and they will run before his chariots. He will appoint for himself commanders of thousands and of fifties, and some to do his plowing and to reap his harvest and to make his weapons of war and equipment for his chariots. He will also take your daughters for perfumers and cooks and bakers. He will take the best of your fields and your vineyards and your olive groves and give them to his servants" (1 Sam. 8:11–14, NASB).

However, the people still demanded a king, and the Lord answered Samuel's prayer and told him to "listen to their voice and appoint them a king" (1 Sam. 8:22, NASB). The first king was Saul from the tribe of Benjamin, who was a "handsome man, and there was not a more handsome person than he among the sons of Israel; from his shoulders and up he was taller than any of the people." (1 Sam. 9:2, NASB). Saul initially obeyed the Lord's will and had many victories in battle over his enemies.

In one memorable battle, the "Philistines stood on the mountain on one side while Israel stood on the mountain on the other side, with the valley between them" (1 Sam. 17:3, NASB). Each day, the Philistine champion named Goliath, who was a giant around nine and a half feet tall would come out of the Philistine camp and shout to the Israelites, "Choose a man for yourselves and let him come down to me. If he is able to fight with me and kill me, then we will become your servants; but if I prevail against him and kill him, then you shall become our servants and serve us" (1 Sam. 17:8–9). Goliath also would say, "This day I defy the armies of Israel! Give me a man and let us fight each other" (1 Sam. 17:10, NASB).

On hearing the Philistine's words, Saul and all the Israelites were dismayed and terrified. One day, David, a shepherd boy from the tribe of Judah with a heart and love for God, came to the battle lines to visit his older brothers. Upon hearing Goliath shouting, David said, "who is this uncircumcised Philistine, that he should taunt the armies of the living God?" (1 Sam. 17:26, NASB). David went to Saul and said,

> "Your servant has killed both the lion and the bear; and this uncircumcised Philistine will be like one of them, since he has taunted the armies of the living God." And David said, "The Lord who delivered me from the paw of the lion and from the paw of the bear, He will deliver me from the hand of this Philistine" (1 Sam. 17:36–37, NASB).

Saul said to David, "Go, and may the Lord be with you" (1 Sam. 17:37, NASB), and he tried to dress David in his armor, but it was too big. David, without armor but with great faith, went out bravely to fight Goliath and said, "You come to me with a sword, a spear, and a javelin, but I come to you in the name of the Lord of hosts, the God of the armies of Israel, whom you have taunted" (1 Sam. 17:45, NASB). Armed only with his sling, David, the shepherd boy, ran toward the heavily armored Goliath, and launched a single rock from his sling, which hit Goliath in the forehead and knocked him down. David then killed Goliath with his own sword to liberate Israel.

Due to this great victory, David was invited into Saul's court and was initially loved by Saul. Overtime, David grew up and became a renowned warrior and Saul became jealous of David. His jealousy turned to hatred and Saul tried to kill David but he avoided capture many times after many close calls. It was during this time period in his reign, where Saul "rejected the word of the Lord" (1 Sam. 15:23, NASB), and because of that the Lord rejected Saul as king. After Saul and his sons were killed by the Philistines, David was anointed king by God, through the prophet Samuel, at the age of thirty-six. David as King of Israel became a great king and warrior. Through the power of God, who David prayed to and consulted before each battle, David earned many important military victories including capturing Salem, which would later become Jerusalem. Over time, David defeated the Philistines, Moabites, Arameans, Edomites, and Ammonites. David loved the Lord God and said, "How great you are, Sovereign Lord! There is no one like you, and there is no God but you" (2 Sam. 7:22). David wrote and dedicated many songs to the Lord and was a man after God's own heart. God told David through the prophet Nathan that "Your house and your kingdom shall endure before Me forever; your throne shall be established forever" (2 Sam. 7:16, NASB).

Temple Worship

King David loved the Lord and wanted to build God a permanent dwelling in a temple rather than the tabernacle, which was a type of tent. However, as David was a warrior, God said that there was too much bloodshed from his hands but "when your days are complete, and you lie down with your fathers, I will raise up your descendant after you, who will come forth from you, and I will establish his kingdom.

He shall build a house for My name, and I will establish the throne of his kingdom forever" (2 Sam. 7:12–13, NASB). After forty years of ruling Israel, David died and was succeeded by his son, Solomon. God appeared to Solomon and said to him, "Ask what you wish Me to give you" (1 Kings 3:5, NASB). Solomon answered God, "Give me wisdom and knowledge, that I may lead this people, for who is able to govern this great people of yours?" (1 Kings 3:9). God said to Solomon,

> "Since you have asked for this and not for long life or wealth for yourself, nor have asked for the death of your enemies but for discernment in administering justice, I will do what you have asked. I will give you a wise and discerning heart, so that there will never have been anyone like you, nor will there ever be. Moreover, I will give you what you have not asked for—both wealth and honor—so that in your lifetime you will have no equal among kings" (1 Kings 3:11–13).

Solomon was then directed by God to build a large ornate temple in Jerusalem on Mount Moriah over the same spot where Abraham was told to sacrifice his son Isaac over a thousand years earlier. To build the temple, Solomon conscripted "laborers from all Israel" (1 Kings 5:13, NASB), including thirty thousand men sent to Lebanon to cut cedar trees for lumber, eighty thousand stonecutters working in the hills, seventy thousand carriers, and thirty-three hundred foremen who supervised the project and directed the workers. The temple was very ornate with "all the walls of the house round about with carved engravings of cherubim, palm trees, and open flowers, inner and outer sanctuaries" and with the floor overlaid "with gold, inner and outer sanctuaries" (1 Kings 6:29–30, NASB). The building of the temple, according to God's instructions, took seven years including an outer court, and an inner court which contained the Altar for burnt offerings, the Holy Place/Sanctuary, and the Holy of Holies. In the Holy Place, there were the Tables of Showbread and the Alters of Incense.

A veil separated the Holy Place from the inner sanctuary called the Holy of Holies in which was placed the Ark of the Covenant.

At the dedication of the temple, King Solomon prayed to the Lord and said the following, "forgive your people, who have sinned against you. Now, my God, may your eyes be open and your ears attentive to the prayers offered in this place. May your priests, Lord God, be clothed with salvation, may your faithful people rejoice in your goodness. Lord God, do not reject your anointed one. Remember the great love promised to David your servant" (2 Chron. 6:39–42). When Solomon finished praying, "fire came down from heaven and consumed the burnt offering and the sacrifices, and the glory of the Lord filled the house" (2 Chron. 7:1, NASB).

Then all of the Israelites "seeing the fire come down and the glory of the Lord upon the house, bowed down on the pavement with their faces to the ground, and they worshiped and gave praise to the Lord, saying, 'Truly He is good, truly His lovingkindness is everlasting'" (2 Chron. 7:3, NASB). With joy and celebration, King Solomon and all of the people "offered sacrifice before the Lord" (2 Chron. 7:4, NASB), which included "a sacrifice of 22,000 oxen and 120,000 sheep" (2 Chron. 7:5, NASB). The Levites with the musical instruments and the priest blew the trumpets and all the people were saying, "His love endures forever" (2 Chron. 7:6). All the people with Solomon celebrated the dedication of the temple for seven days and then continued the festival for seven days more.

Each year afterward, the temple was used to cover the sins of the people through animal sacrifices on a specific day called the Day of Atonement. For this sacrifice, unblemished male lambs and goats, without defect, were carefully chosen. The high priest would put his hand upon the animal's head, he would confess his sins and those of the people, and then would pray that all the sins of the Israelites and the punishment for those sins would be transferred to the animal, which would then be killed. Only the high priest could enter the Holy of Holies and would sprinkle the blood of the animals to intercede for the sins of the people. The blood of the animals, which was considered the life, was the vital part of the sacrifice and its sprinkling of the blood was the acceptable offer to God for atonement/ covering of the sins of the people.

Destruction of the Northern Kingdom

After King Solomon died, the kingdom of Israel was split into two kingdoms with the ten Northern tribes forming the nation of Israel, and the two Southern tribes forming the nation of Judah. While Solomon's kingdom was very strong and God provided rest for the land, in the divided kingdom, there were many wars between Israel and Judah and also with their neighbors. The result was that both kingdoms over time were weakened significantly. The remainder of the period of the Kings was a cyclical story similar to the time of Judges with good kings often followed by bad kings. The good kings obeyed God and stopped the worshiping of false idols, including Baal and Asherah, and removed the high places of pagan worship from the land. The bad kings allowed idolatry and worship of the many pagan gods from the cultures surrounding Israel and would reestablish the high places of false worship, thus removing God's blessing and assuring his wrath. Due to their continual disobedience, God allowed the ten tribes of Israel to be conquered by the Assyrians around 722 BC and the survivors were taken out of the land to Assyria as prisoners and slaves.

The Assyrian advance continued through the Southern Kingdom of Judah and all the way to the walls of Jerusalem. At Jerusalem's walls, Sennacherib, the King of Assyria, mocked the Israelites saying "Has any one of the gods of the nations delivered his land from the hand of the king of Assyria? Where are the gods of Hamath and Arpad? Where are the gods of Sepharvaim, Hena and Ivvah? Have they delivered Samaria from my hand? Who among all the gods of the lands have delivered their land from my hand, that the Lord should deliver Jerusalem from my hand?" (2 Kings 18:33–35, NASB). In response, the obedient and good King Hezekiah of Judah tore his clothes and Hezekiah along with all the people repented of their sins and put on sackcloth and prayed for deliverance.

The Lord answered King Hezekiah's prayers through the prophet Isaiah and said this about the king of Assyria, "'Whom have you reproached and blasphemed? And against whom have you raised your voice, And haughtily lifted up your eyes? Against the Holy One of Israel!" (2 Kings 19:22, NASB). The Lord also said, "Because of your raging against Me, And because your arrogance has come up to My ears, Therefore I will put My hook in your nose, And My bridle in your lips, And I will turn you back by the way which you came" (2 Kings 19:28, NASB). The Lord further declared, "For I will defend this city to save it for My own sake and for My servant David's sake" (2 Kings 19:34, NASB).

Later that night "the angel of the Lord went out and struck 185,000 in the camp of the Assyrians; and when men rose early in the morning, behold, all of them were dead. So Sennacherib king of Assyria departed and returned home" (2 Kings 19:35–36, NASB). After Sennacherib, with the remaining soldiers, left Jerusalem and headed back to Assyria, they would never return and threaten Judah again.

Destruction of the Southern Kingdom and the Time of Exile

Judah, the Southern Kingdom, was spared destruction due to the Israelites repentance during the time of King Hezekiah. But as time progressed, Judah continued the cycle of good kings who removed idols and obeyed God followed often by bad kings who rebelled against God and worshiped the gods and idols of the neighboring peoples. During these times of disobedience, God sent prophets to the people to have them repent of their sins and return to him. During the fall of the Northern Kingdom, prophets including Isaiah and Hosea were sent, and during the time of the fall of the Southern Kingdom, prophets including Jeremiah and Habakkuk were present and prophesizing.

King Zedekiah's reign in the Southern Kingdom started around 575 BC, but "he did evil in the sight of the Lord his God; he did not humble himself before Jeremiah the prophet who spoke for the Lord" (2 Chron. 36:12, NASB). King Zedekiah "stiffened his neck and hardened his heart against turning to the Lord God of Israel. Furthermore, all the officials of the priests and the people were very unfaithful following all the abominations of the nations; and they defiled the house of the Lord which He had sanctified in Jerusalem" (2 Chron. 36:13–14, NASB). Furthermore, "they continually mocked the messengers of God, despised His words and scoffed at His prophets, until the wrath of the Lord arose against His people, until there was no remedy" (2 Chron. 36:16, NASB).

In response to their disobedience, God raised up Nebuchadnezzar, who became the king of the Babylonians. The Babylonians defeated the Assyrians to become the world power, and in the year 586 BC, they conquered the land of Judah including Jerusalem. Nebuchadnezzar's armies "slew their young men with the sword in the house of their sanctuary, and had no compassion on young man or virgin, old man or infirm; He gave them all into his hand. All the articles of the house of God, great and small, and the treasures of the house of the Lord, and the treasures of the king and of his officers, he brought them all to Babylon. Then they burned the house of God and broke down the wall of Jerusalem, and burned all its fortified buildings with fire and destroyed all its valuable articles. Those who had escaped from the sword he carried away to Babylon; and they were servants to him and to his sons" (2 Chron. 36:17–19, NASB).

During their time in exile in Babylon and later in Media Persia after Babylon was destroyed, God did not abandon the Israelites, but instead raised up prophets including Ezekiel, Daniel, and Zechariah, who prophesized to the Israelites. Moreover, often these prophets were greatly blessed and rose up to high levels of authority as trusted administrators and advisors to the various kings. These prophets of God were often given gifts and special abilities in order to predict future events, interpret dreams, and provide wise and discerning judgment.

Return to the Promised Land

While the remnants of the Israelites were in exile, it may have seemed that God had broken his promise with Abraham that he would be a father "of a great nation" (Gen. 12:2) or his promise to King David that "your throne shall be established forever" (2 Sam. 7:16, NASB). However, despite being slaves in captivity, God kept a faithful remnant alive and protected of each Israelite tribe. The prophet Isaiah, through the word of God, predicted about eighty years before Judah was taken into captivity that God would use "Cyrus His anointed" (Isa. 45:1, NASB) and that Cyrus "will build My city and will let My exiles go free" (Isa. 45:13, NASB). As predicted by the Lord, after being in Babylon for seventy years, the exiles were allowed to return to the Promised Land through King Cyrus of the Media Persian Empire and would rebuild Jerusalem. The exiles, over fifty thousand in number, returned over a hundred-year period and were led by the prophets Zerubbabel, Ezra, and Nehemiah. Zerubbabel led the group of exiles that rebuilt the destroyed temple and the altar. Ezra reestablished the religious principles, which preexisted prior to the exile, and ceremonial sacrifice and worship to God were restarted. Nehemiah rebuilt the destroyed city wall around Jerusalem and houses were reestablished and Jerusalem was once again inhabited.

During this period of rebuilding, the exiles—who had returned—were often harassed and threatened by their neighbors. Nehemiah records that "those who carried materials did their work with one hand and held a weapon in the other, and each of the build-ers wore his sword at his side as he worked" (Neh. 4:17–18). Thus, the Israelites were under great duress with enemies on all sides, but through faith conquered their fears and completed their tasks. After the major rebuilding ended, the Israelites began living full time within the city walls of Jerusalem and worshiped in the second temple on Mount Moriah, which while rebuilt was only a fraction of its former glory. The rebuilding of the temple to form the very large Temple Mount complex would continue periodically for the next five hun-dred years and would not be completed until the time of King Herod.

The Silent Period

Malachi was the last prophet as recorded in the book of Malachi (i.e., the last book of the Old Testament), and afterward, there was a Silent Period in Israel's history, which lasted for over four hundred years. During this time period, there were no recorded prophets sent by God and no inspired writings. This Silent Period was predicted over 550 years earlier during the time of King David in the following passage, "We are given no signs from God; no prophets are left, and none of us knows how long this will be" (Ps. 74:9).

History records that indeed this was a very difficult time in the land of Israel as there were many successive invasions by many foreign rulers, which included the Persians, Greeks, Ptolemy's, Seleucids, and Romans. From this long period of almost constant war and oppression, and seemingly abandoned by God (they were not), the Jews were eagerly seeking the appearance of the Messiah/Christ, who they believed, would rescue them from their oppressors, including later on from their Roman rulers.

The people expected the Messiah would come as a conquering king who "will go forth and fight against those nations, as when He fights on a day of battle" (Zech. 14:3, NASB). The Messiah's kingdom would be "given authority, glory and sovereign power" and "all nations and peoples of every language" would worship him and that the Messiah's dominion would be "an everlasting dominion that will not pass away" and his kingdom would be one "that will never be destroyed" (Dan. 7:14).

However, while not fully understood at the time, before the Messiah was to come as a conquering king, Scripture revealed that the Messiah was first to come as a sacrificial lamb "to restore the preserved ones of Israel" and to be "a light of the nations So that My salvation may reach to the end of the earth" (Isa. 49:6, NASB). Additionally, in advance of the coming of the Messiah, it is recorded that the Lord Almighty would send his "messenger, who will prepare the way before me" (Mal. 3:1). While not known how long the Silent Period would last, the timing of the ending of this period was prophesized by the prophet Micah in the following passages.

"But you, Bethlehem Ephrathah, though you are small among the clans of Judah, out of you will come for me one who will be ruler over Israel, whose origins are from of old, from ancient times. Therefore Israel will be abandoned until the time when she who is in labor bears a son, and the rest of his brothers return to join the Israelites" (Mic. 5:2–3).

The Birth of Christ

Before the Messiah was to come, it was predicted that God would send his *messenger* and also that he would be "a voice of one calling in the wilderness" (Isa. 40:3). John the Baptist was born over six months before the Messiah and fulfilled prophecy as the *messenger*. John baptized in the Jordan River and became a powerful prophet in the Judean wilderness "preaching a baptism of repentance for the forgiveness of sins" (Luke 3:3, NASB). John predicted the coming of Jesus and said, "I baptize you with water for repentance, but He who is coming after me is mightier than I, and I am not fit to remove His sandals; He will baptize you with the Holy Spirit and fire. His winnowing fork is in His hand, and He will thoroughly clear His threshing floor; and He will gather His wheat into the barn, but He will burn up the chaff with unquenchable fire" (Matt. 3:11–12, NASB).

During this time, in Nazareth, there was a young woman named Mary who was betrothed but not yet married to her husband Joseph. Both Mary and Joseph were from the tribe of Judah. One day, an angel came to Mary and said,

> "'Do not be afraid, Mary; for you have found favor with God. And behold, you will conceive in your womb and bear a son, and you shall name Him Jesus. He will be great and will be called the Son of the Most High; and the Lord God will give Him the throne of His father David; and He will reign over the house of Jacob forever, and His kingdom will have no end.' Mary said to the angel, 'How can this be, since I am a virgin?' The

angel answered and said to her, 'The Holy Spirit will come upon you, and the power of the Most High will overshadow you; and for that reason the holy Child shall be called the Son of God'" (Luke 1:30–35, NASB).

Mary answered, "I am the Lord's servant" and that "May your word to me be fulfilled" (Luke 1:38).

While having to take part in a census dictated by the Roman rulers, Joseph and Mary traveled from Nazareth in the Galilee region to Bethlehem, which is near Jerusalem. At Bethlehem, since the inn was full, Jesus, the son of God, who was conceived by Mary and the Holy Spirit, was born in a manger. This birth was predicted by the inspired words of the prophet Isaiah over seven hundred years earlier when he wrote, "Behold, a virgin will be with child and bear a son, and she will call His name Immanuel"—Immanuel means God with us (Isa. 7:14, NASB).

After Jesus was born, an angel appeared to shepherds living out in the fields nearby and announced, "Do not be afraid; for behold, I bring you good news of great joy which will be for all the people; for today in the city of David there has been born for you a Savior, who is Christ the Lord" (Luke 2:10–11, NASB). After this "a great company of the heavenly host appeared with the angel, praising God and saying, Glory to God in the highest heaven, and on earth peace to those on whom his favor rests" (Luke 2:13–14).

Jesus's exact lineage was recorded in the Bible and "all the generations from Abraham to David are fourteen generations; from David to the deportation to Babylon, fourteen generations; and from the deportation to Babylon to the Messiah, fourteen generations" (Matt. 1:17, NASB). A few days after the birth, Joseph and Mary took the newborn Jesus to the temple in Jerusalem, according to the customs of the Jews, to be consecrated to the Lord. There was a righteous and devout man living in Jerusalem, names Simeon, whom the Holy Spirit had told him many years earlier that he would not die until he had seen the Lord's Messiah. Upon seeing the baby Jesus, Simeon declared, "For my eyes have seen Your salvation, Which You have prepared in the presence of all peoples, A Light of revelation to the Gentiles, And the glory of Your people Israel" (Luke 2:30–32, NASB). After this, he warned, "Behold, this Child is appointed for the fall and rise of many in Israel, and for a sign to be opposed— and a sword will pierce even your own soul—to the end that thoughts from many hearts may be revealed" (Luke 2:34–35, NASB).

The Life of Christ

During the time period of Christ's birth, Herod, an Edomite by birth, was appointed King of Judea by the Roman Empire. Herod was a power hungry individual and because of this was extremely paranoid about losing his kingdom bestowed upon him by the Romans. One day, Magi (i.e., wise men) from the East came to Herod to inquire about the new King of the Jews as they had seen a star announcing his birth and wanted to know where to worship him. Alarmed, Herod called in the chief priests and teachers of the law and found out that the Messiah would be born in Bethlehem in Judea. He told the Magi to go there but afterward to come back and report to him. The Magi went to Bethlehem and found the baby Jesus and "fell to the ground and worshiped Him" and "opening their treasures, they presented to Him gifts of gold, frankincense, and myrrh" (Matt. 2:11, NASB).

The Magi were then "warned by God in a dream not to return to Herod" (Matt. 2:12, NASB) and thus returned to their homeland by another way. After some time had passed, Herod learned that he had been tricked by the Magi and that they were gone. Herod then "became very enraged, and sent and slew all the male children who were in Bethlehem and all its vicinity, from two years old and under" (Matt. 2:16, NASB). However, Joseph had already been warned in a dream by an angel to leave Nazareth and had escaped with Mary and Jesus to Egypt. Several years later, after Herod's death, Joseph was again confronted by an angel in his dream, and was told to "go into the land of Israel; for those who sought the Child's life are dead" (Matt. 2:20, NASB).

Little is recorded about Jesus childhood other then he grew up in the Galilee region in the city of Nazareth as a carpenter/stone mason, which was his father's trade. Jesus lived a normal life in that period of time but, as he grew, it was recorded that he "become strong, increasing in wisdom; and the grace of God was upon Him" (Luke 2:40, NASB). It is known that Jesus traveled once a year with his family to celebrate the Passover in Jerusalem according to the customs of the day. When Jesus was twelve and considered an adult in the Jewish law, he was left behind accidently by his parents who had left Jerusalem. Upon returning, they "found Him in the temple, sitting in the midst of the teachers, both listening to them and asking them questions" and "all who heard Him were amazed at His understanding and His answers" (Luke 2:46–47, NASB).

When Jesus was "about thirty years of age," Jesus was baptized by John the Baptist in the Jordan River (Luke 3:23, NASB). At this time, "after being baptized, Jesus came up immediately from the water; and behold, the heavens were opened, and he saw the Spirit of God descending as a dove and lighting on Him, and behold, a voice out of the heavens said, 'This is My beloved Son, in whom I am well-pleased'" (Matt. 3:16–17, NASB). Soon afterward, Jesus was led by the Spirit into the wilderness to fast and during this time he was tempted by Satan. At his weakest point after fasting for forty days, Satan said to him, "If You are the Son of God, command that these stones become bread" (Matt. 4:3, NASB). Jesus answered, "It is written, Man shall not live on bread alone, but on every word that proceeds out of the mouth of God" (Matt. 4:4, NASB). Amongst other things, Satan offered Jesus all of the kingdoms of the world if he would bow down to him. Jesus refused and rebuked Satan by quoting Scripture, "When the devil had finished every temptation, he left Him until an opportune time" (Luke 4:13, NASB).

The Ministry of Christ

To start his ministry, Jesus called twelve disciples to follow him including Peter (Simon), Andrew, James, John, Philip, Bartholomew, Matthew, Thomas, James (son of Alphaeus), Simon, Judas (son of James), and Judas Iscariot—who would later betray Jesus. Jesus told his disciples, "Behold, I send you out as sheep in the midst of wolves;

so be shrewd as serpents and innocent as doves" (Matt. 10:26, NASB). Jesus also told them to "proclaim this message: The kingdom of heaven has come near" (Matt. 10:7), and "do not fear those who kill the body but are unable to kill the soul; but rather fear Him who is able to destroy both soul and body in hell" (Matt. 10:28, NASB).

During his ministry, Jesus often stayed in Capernaum along the Sea of Galilee in the house of Peter, one of his disciples. Jesus taught in the synagogues and also met with and talked to the people directly. He often explained Scripture (i.e., the Old Testament) and key concepts about God's kingdom by using parables. When Jesus spoke, he spoke not as just a man or a prophet, but "crowds were amazed at his teaching, because he taught as one who had authority, and not as their teachers of the law" (Matt. 7:28–29). Jesus also brought a message much different than the Jewish religious leaders. Jesus's teaching was not focused on religious ceremonies and the penalties of the Law, but a ministry focused on love and on a personal relationship with God. Jesus talked about blessings and that those that the world considered blessed would be cursed and those that would be considered cursed would be blessed. Often, Jesus brought his teaching and miracles, not to those considered blessed, but to the sick, the weak, and the social outcasts including those that were physically unclean with various diseases and those who were not ethnically pure.

An example of Jesus's teaching is the sermon that Jesus gave on the Mount of Beatitudes, located nearby the Sea of Galilee. Jesus brought a new type of humility in his teaching and the sermon's first ten verses are the following, "Blessed are the poor in spirit, for theirs is the kingdom of heaven. Blessed are those who mourn, for they shall be comforted. Blessed are the gentle, for they shall inherit the earth. Blessed are those who hunger and thirst for righteousness, for they shall be satisfied. Blessed are the merciful, for they shall receive mercy. Blessed are the pure in heart, for they shall see God. Blessed are the peacemakers, for they shall be called sons of God. Blessed are those who have been persecuted for the sake of righteousness, for theirs is the kingdom of heaven. Blessed are you when people insult you and persecute you, and falsely say all kinds of evil against you because of Me. Rejoice and be glad, for your reward in heaven is great; for in the same way they persecuted the prophets who were before you" (Matt. 5:3–12, NASB).

Jesus exhibited authority over nature, over demons, and over death. As predicted by prophecy, Jesus performed many signs and miracles including those described in the following passage; "the blind receive sight, the lame walk, the lepers are cleansed, and the deaf hear, the dead are raised up, the poor have the gospel preached to them" (Luke 7:22, NASB). Jesus cared greatly for the children, the poor, the sinners, and the downtrodden. Scripture reveals that "Jesus wept" (John 11:35, NASB) when he heard about his friend Lazarus's death, who he later raised from the dead. In spite of Jesus's love for the people, Jesus was generally hated by the Hebrew religious leaders, which included the Pharisees, Sadducees, and teachers of the law.

These *leaders* had risen to prominent positions in Jewish society and their false piety and onerous teaching of the Law had put a heavy burden on the people. To expose their sinful ways, Jesus told the parable of the tax collector in the following verses,

> "Two men went up into the temple to pray, one a Pharisee and the other a tax collector. The Pharisee stood and was praying this to himself: 'God, I thank You that I am not like other people: swindlers, unjust, adulterers, or even like this tax collector. I fast twice a week; I pay tithes of all that I get. But the tax collector, standing some distance away, was even unwilling to lift up his eyes to heaven, but was beating his breast, saying, 'God, be merciful to me, the sinner!' I tell you, this man went to his house justified rather than the other; for everyone who exalts himself will be humbled, but he who humbles himself will be exalted" (Luke 18:10–14, NASB).

Scripture records many instances where Jesus declared that he was God. While in Samaria, Jesus met a Samaritan woman at a well and during the following discussion, he said, "Everyone who drinks of this water will thirst again; but whoever drinks of the water that I will give him shall never thirst; but the water that I will give him will become in him a well of water springing up to eternal life" (John 4:13–14, NASB). The Samaritan woman said to Him, "I know that Messiah is coming (He who is called Christ); when that One comes, He will declare all things to us.' Jesus said to her, 'I who speak to you am He'" (John 4:25–26, NASB).

Jesus replied at different times to others that "I and the Father are one" (John 10:30), "I am God's Son" (John 10:36), and "I am he." (John 18:5). While in the temple courts, the Jews questioned his authority and demanded that Jesus provide a miraculous sign. Jesus, speaking of himself, answered, "Destroy this temple, and I will raise it again in three days" (John 2:19). Because Jesus clearly claimed to be God, God's son, and the Messiah (he was indeed all of these), the high priests accused Jesus of blasphemy for claiming to be God and tried to stone him and further plotted to kill him.

The Betrayal and Capture of Christ

While experiencing all manner of temptations while living on the earth as a man, Jesus did not sin and lived a sinless life. Just prior to the yearly Passover celebration, Jesus rode into Jerusalem on a donkey as predicted by the prophet Zechariah over five hundred years earlier;

> "Rejoice greatly, O daughter of Zion! Shout in triumph, O daughter of Jerusalem! Behold, your king is coming to you; He is just and endowed with salvation, Humble, and mounted on a donkey." (Zech. 9:9, NASB). The crowds gathered as Jesus rode and shouted, "Hosanna to the Son of David; Blessed is HE who comes in the name of the Lord" (Matt. 21:9, NASB).

"When He had entered Jerusalem, all the city was stirred, saying, 'Who is this?' And the crowds were saying, 'This is the prophet

Jesus, from Nazareth in Galilee'" (Matt. 21:10–11). While initially treated like a king by the people, this treatment would be short-lived, and due to the hatred from the Pharisees and the influence of Satan, the people would soon turn against Jesus.

Outside of the city walls that evening, Jesus had dinner with his disciples, and during this time predicted that this would be his *last supper* and said, "I shall never again eat it until it is fulfilled in the kingdom of God" (Luke 22:16, NASB). Jesus took the bread, gave thanks and broke it, and gave it to them, saying, "This is My body which is given for you; do this in remembrance of Me.' And in the same way He took the cup after they had eaten, saying, 'This cup which is poured out for you is the new covenant in My blood" (Luke 22:19–20, NASB). During dinner, Jesus predicted that he would be betrayed by one of his disciples, Judas Iscariot. Soon afterward, Satan entered Judas and Jesus said to him, "What you do, do quickly" (John 13:27, NASB).

After dinner, Jesus and his disciples, minus Judas Iscariot, went across the Kidron Valley and partially up the Mount of Olives to a grove of olive trees, which is called the Garden of Gethsemane. In great agony for the task ahead, Jesus's "sweat was like drops of blood" (Luke 22:44), and he prayed earnestly to the Father "if it is not possible for this cup to be taken away unless I drink it, may your will be done" (Matt. 26:42). Jesus continued in earnest prayer, "Father, if you are willing, take this cup from me; yet not my will, but yours be done" (Luke 22:42). Jesus's cup was the cup of the new covenant related to his dying for the sins of all mankind, which would happen after his crucifixion on the cross that he knew must soon be endured.

After praying, while still in Gethsemane, a crowd armed with swords and clubs along with armed soldiers came to arrest Jesus. Judas Iscariot was among them and went up to Jesus and signaled to the guards who Jesus was by giving him a kiss. As the soldiers attempted to arrest Jesus, Jesus asked, "Who is it you want" (John 18:4), and they replied "Jesus of Nazareth" (John 18:5). "When Jesus said, 'I am he,' they drew back and fell to the ground" (John 18:6) as they were totally overwhelmed being in the presence of God. Peter, a disciple, attempted to defend Jesus and, with a mighty but misguided blow, cut off the ear of the servant of the High Priest with a sword. Jesus commanded Peter, "Put your sword away! Shall I not drink the cup the Father has given me?" (John 18:11).

Then Jesus touched the man's ear and healed him. Jesus told Peter, after he tried to defend Jesus, "Do you think I cannot call on my Father, and he will at once put at my disposal more than twelve legions of angels? But how then would the Scriptures be fulfilled that say it must happen in this way?" (Matt. 26:53–54). Jesus thus let himself be captured, and he was bound by the guards and led away while the disciples scattered.

The Judgment and Death of Christ

After his capture, Jesus was brought before the high Priest Caiaphas and the teachers of the law for questioning and accusation. Caiaphas said,

> "I charge you under oath by the living God: Tell us if you are the Messiah, the Son of God.' 'You have said so,' Jesus replied. 'But I say to all of you: From now on you will see the Son of Man sitting at the right hand of the Mighty One and coming on the clouds of heaven.' Then the high priest tore his clothes and said, 'He has spoken blasphemy!" (Matt. 26:63–65).

The entire assembly then brought him before Pontius Pilate, who was the Roman governor of Judea. After questioning Jesus, Pilate said, "I find no basis for a charge against this man." (Luke 23:4).

After learning that he was from Galilee, Pilate sent him to Herod (Antipas), the ruler of the Galilee region. However, after questioning Jesus, Herod sent him back to Pilate. Pilate brought together, the chief priests, the rulers and the people and said, "I have examined him in your presence and have found no basis for your charges against him. Neither has Herod, for he sent him back to us; as you can see, he has done nothing to deserve death. Therefore, I will punish him and then release him" (Luke 23:14–16). Pilate, after finding no fault in Jesus, next attempted to let him go according to a tradition during the time of the Passover, as the Roman governor would let the people decide on setting one prisoner free. Pilate gave the people the choice of Barabbas, a dangerous revolutionary or Jesus. The people chose Barabbas to set free and then "kept shouting about Jesus, "Crucify him! Crucify him!" (Luke 23:20). Pilate was perplexed and

> "for the third time he spoke to them: 'Why? What crime has this man committed? I have found in him no grounds for the death penalty. Therefore I will have him punished and then release him.' But with loud shouts they insistently demanded that he be crucified, and their shouts prevailed. So Pilate decided to grant their demand" (Luke 23:22–24).

After Pilate's order, Jesus was very severely treated and was first flogged with a cat of nine tails, which is a whip with metal shards at the end. Next, he was very severely beaten, mocked by the guards, and a crown of thorns was thrust on his head. Finally, after an agonizing journey to the place of the skull called Golgotha (or Calvary), Jesus was crucified along with two sinners. Crucifixion was done by hammering large iron spikes through the base of each hand and one through both feet onto a large cross-shaped beam. During the crucifixion, Jesus said, "Father, forgive them, for they do not know what they are doing" (Luke 23:34). After the crucifixion, Jesus was hauled up onto the pole, which was placed vertically in the ground. Fastened to Jesus's cross by order of Pilate was a sign written in Aramaic, Latin, and Greek, which read "Jesus of Nazareth, the King of the Jews" (John 19:19).

While dying on the cross, one of the sinners crucified with Jesus was belligerent and unrepentant. But the other sinner was repentant and asked for forgiveness. Jesus told the repentant sinner, "Truly I tell you, today you will be with me in paradise" (Luke 23:43). Around the middle of the day, the sun stopped shining, and darkness came over the entire land for three hours from approximately nine to noon. Later, knowing that everything had now been finished, and that Scripture would be fulfilled, Jesus said, "It is finished" (John 19:30).

Soon afterward, Jesus bowed his head and gave up his spirit. Scripture records that "at that moment the curtain of the temple was torn in two from top to bottom. The earth shook, the rocks split, and the tombs broke open" (Matt. 27:51–52). "When the centurion and those with him who were guarding Jesus saw the earthquake and all that had happened, they were terrified, and exclaimed, 'Surely he was the Son of God!'" (Matt. 27:54). The Roman guards examined Jesus and found him dead but to be absolutely sure, "One of the soldiers pierced Jesus's side with a spear, bringing a sudden flow of blood and water" (John 19:34). Additionally, the soldiers "broke the legs of the first man who had been crucified with Jesus, and then those of the other" (John 19:32). This resulted in both of their deaths a short time later.

After the death of Jesus, Joseph of Arimathea asked Pontius Pilate for the body of Jesus and was granted permission. Joseph and Nicodemus, a Pharisee, took Jesus's body down from the cross and then took his body to a nearby garden wherein there was a "new tomb, in which no one had ever been laid" (John 19:41). A large rock was rolled in front of the tomb. During this time, the chief priests and the Pharisees went to Pilate to ask that the tomb be heavily guarded. "Take a guard', Pilate answered, 'Go, make the tomb as secure as you know how.' So they went and made the tomb secure by putting a seal on the stone and posting the guard'" (Matt. 27:65–66).

The Resurrection of Christ

After three days had passed, women who were followers of Jesus went to the tomb with anointing spices. As they approached the tomb, there

> "was a violent earthquake, for an angel of
> the Lord came down from heaven and, going to

the tomb, rolled back the stone and sat on it. His appearance was like lightning, and his clothes were white as snow. The guards were so afraid of him that they shook and became like dead men. The angel said to the women, 'Do not be afraid, for I know that you are looking for Jesus, who was crucified. He is not here; he has risen, just as he said. Come and see the place where he lay. Then go quickly and tell his disciples: 'He has risen from the dead and is going ahead of you into Galilee" (Matt. 28:2–7).

Afterward, the women left hurriedly and ran to tell Jesus's disciples. After being told, the apostles, John and Peter, raced to the empty tomb. Upon arriving, they saw the strips of burial linen lying by themselves and the empty tomb and then reported this back to the other disciples.

The resurrected Christ next appeared to two pilgrims on the road to Emmaus, which is a town not far from Jerusalem. While walking with them, "Beginning with Moses and all the prophets," Jesus then "explained to them what was said in all the Scriptures concerning himself" (Luke 24:27). Later on, Jesus appeared to all of the disciples at one time, other than Judas Iscariot who had committed suicide, and Thomas who was absent. Jesus said, "Peace be with you" (Luke 24:36), and that "this is what I told you while I was still with you: Everything must be fulfilled that is written about me in the Law of Moses, the Prophets and the Psalms" (Luke 24:44). Then Jesus "opened their minds, so they could understand the Scriptures. He told them, "This is what is written: The Messiah will suffer and rise from the dead on the third day, and repentance for the forgiveness of sins will be preached in his name to all nations, beginning at Jerusalem" (Luke 24:45–47).

Upon hearing of this visit from the other disciples, Thomas (who would later be referred to as *Doubting Thomas*) said that he would not believe until he sees and feels the holes in Jesus's hands and the hole in Jesus's side where the spear was thrust. A week later,

Jesus appeared to all of the disciples including Thomas and said to Thomas,

> "'Put your finger here; see my hands. Reach out your hand and put it into my side. Stop doubting and believe.' Thomas said to him, 'My Lord and My God!'" (John 20:27–28).

In addition to these recorded incidents, Jesus appeared in his resurrected body to many witnesses, including to more than five hundred men and women at the same time. After appearing to various people over a forty-day period, Jesus appeared on top of the Mount of Olives and told his disciples that "all authority in heaven and on earth has been given to me. Therefore go and make disciples of all nations, baptizing them in the name of the Father, and of the Son, and of the Holy Spirit" (Matt. 28:18–19). Jesus then ascended into heaven in a cloud.

The Spread of the Good News

Before ascending into heaven, Jesus told the disciples that "I am sending forth the promise of My Father upon you; but you are to stay in the city until you are clothed with power from on high" (Luke 24:49, NASB). On the fiftieth day after the Passover, the Feast of Weeks occurred, which is a religious holiday celebrated to give thanksgiving to the Lord. On this day, as the disciples were gathered together, "suddenly a sound like the blowing of a violent wind came from heaven and filled the whole house where they were sitting. They saw what seemed to be tongues of fire that separated and came to rest on each of them. All of them were filled with the Holy Spirit and began to speak in other tongues as the Spirit enabled them" (Acts 2:2–4). This noise attracted a large crowd from many nations, and they were "utterly amazed" (Acts 2:7), for each one to hear their own language being spoken. That first day, three thousand of the crowd were baptized and became believers, and "the Lord added to their number daily those who were being saved" (Acts 2:47).

While being persecuted, the disciples spread out to provide the good news of the gospel (i.e., the birth, death, and resurrection of Christ) to the known world. A Pharisee named Saul was one of the many persecutors of the new Christians (i.e., followers of Christ). Saul was especially zealous in this pursuit and "began to destroy the church. Going from house to house, he dragged off both men and women and put them in prison" (Acts 8:3). Saul additionally oversaw and approved of the stoning of Stephen, a follower of Christ, outside of the gates of Jerusalem.

One day, while searching for Christians to take as prisoners, Saul saw a powerful vision with light flashing from heaven and fell to the ground. He "heard a voice say 'Saul, why do you persecute me?' 'Who are you, Lord?' Saul asked and Jesus replied, 'I am Jesus, whom you are persecuting'" (Acts 9:4–5). Saul then became blind and was taken to Damascus. In Damascus, the Lord sent Ananias, a disciple, to go to Saul and "placing his hands on Saul, he said, 'Brother Saul, the Lord—Jesus, who appeared to you on the road as you were coming here—has sent me so that you may see again and be filled with the Holy Spirit.' Immediately, something like scales fell from Saul's eyes, and he could see again. He got up and was baptized" (Acts 9:17–18). After this, "Saul grew more and more powerful and baffled the Jews living in Damascus by proving that Jesus is the Messiah" (Acts 9:22).

Saul, who accepted Christ, was transformed and renamed by God as Paul, and would become the inspired writer of much of the New Testament. Paul was a Pharisee and could be considered a "Hebrew of Hebrews" (Phil. 3:5) with a perfect Jewish background and lineage through the tribe of Benjamin. After many Jews rejected his message, Paul focused his ministry on the Gentiles as the Lord had commanded, "I have made you a light for the Gentiles, that you may bring salvation to the ends of the earth" (Acts 13:47). With the conversion of Saul and the growth of this ministry, "the church throughout Judea, Galilee and Samaria enjoyed a time of peace and was strengthened. Living in the power of the Lord and encouraged by the Holy Spirit, it increased in numbers" (Acts 9:31).

The establishment of the Christian Church occurred in the perfect time in history as the Romans had established a forced peace throughout the region and had built an extensive network of roads covering tens of thousands of miles. These factors assisted in the word of the Lord being spread through the whole region through Paul, Peter, and John along with the other disciples resulting in an ever-increasing numbers of Christian believers. Today, the gospel message is still being preached throughout the world, and Christianity is still expanding towards fulfilling Jesus's words that "this gospel of the kingdom will be preached in the whole world as a testimony to all nations" (Matt. 24:14).

Chapter 6

Understanding History's Design

It may seem strange to think of history as historical design but God, who is in complete control of his creation, directed history to weave one consistent story covering at least four thousand years and then also ensured that key events of this history were recorded and preserved in Scripture. The *Biblical History of the Universe*, provided in the previous chapter, may seem to be a collection of stories, which are about separate isolated events. However, the entirety of Biblical history can be related to the birth, life, death, and resurrection of the Messiah, who is Jesus Christ. While in Jerusalem two thousand years ago, Jesus told the Jewish religious leaders, "You study the Scriptures diligently because you think that in them you have eternal life. These are the very Scriptures that testify about me." (John 5:39). The climax of history was the most important event to ever occur in history, which was the death of Jesus Christ on the cross. Jesus said while dying on the cross, "It is finished" and after that "he bowed his head and gave up his spirit" (John 19:30). *Finished* didn't mean that the world or time had come to end or that there was not a lot of work yet remaining in order to "bring salvation to the ends of the earth" (Acts 13:47). *Finished* means completed in the sense that God's plan from ancient days, as described in the Old Testament Scripture, was fulfilled resulting in the completion of a pathway of salvation through Christ's death on the cross.

In the Bible, the most famous passage of Scripture is John 3:16. To understand *History's Design* and the reason for key events throughout the Old Testament, one can study six verses only which surround John 3:16 specifically versus 13 through 18. These key verses, which will be broken down and explained linking Old Testament and New Testament events, are the following with the verse number highlighted from John chapter 3:

> *13* "No one has ever gone into heaven except the one who came from heaven—the Son of Man."
>
> *14* "Just as Moses lifted up the snake in the wilderness, so the Son of Man must be lifted up,"
>
> *15* "that everyone who believes may have eternal life in him."
>
> *16* "For God so loved the world that he gave his one and only Son, that whoever believes in him shall not perish but have eternal life."
>
> *17* "For God did not send his Son into the world to condemn the world, but to save the world through him."
>
> *18* "Whoever believes in him is not condemned, but whoever does not believe stands condemned already because they have not believed in the name of God's one and only Son."

By examining each of these verses in more detail, a great understanding of God's will and sovereignty on the design of history can be understood.

13 "No one has ever gone into heaven except the one who came from heaven—the Son of Man."

In a discussion with the Jewish religious leaders, Jesus asked them, "What do you think about the Messiah? Whose son is he?' 'The son of David,' they replied. He said to them, 'How is it then that David, speaking by the Spirit, calls him 'Lord'? For he says, 'The Lord said to my Lord: 'Sit at my right hand until I put your enemies under your feet.' If then David calls him 'Lord,' how can he be his son?" (Matt. 22:41–45). This was a very perplexing question that the Pharisees could not answer since the *son of David* signifies a genealogical lineage coming after David, and *Lord* signifies a master, superior, or elder representing someone living before David.

This answer is clear through the lens of Christ as described in the following passages with reference to Jesus clarified by the added brackets; "In the beginning was the Word (Jesus), and the Word (Jesus) was with God, and the Word (Jesus) was God. He (Jesus) was with God in the beginning" (John 1:1–3), and "The Word (Jesus) became flesh and made his dwelling among us" (John 1:14). Thus, Jesus, as God, has lived forever and was present when the earth and the universe were made. Thus, Jesus is the Lord of all including Lord to King David.

Jesus is also the Son of Man with respect to his birth on the earth, which occurred more than a thousand years after David. With respect to genealogy, Jesus, as a man, is a direct descendant of David through both Mary (his Mother) and Joseph (his non biological father). The birth of Jesus Christ into the tribe of Judah, through the line of David, fulfilled the prophecy from the prophet Jeremiah that "David will never fail to have a man to sit on the throne of Israel" (Jer. 33:17). Jesus died on the cross, was resurrected, and then ascended back into heaven to his eternal kingdom. By doing so, Jesus fulfilled the prophecy of Nathan, the prophet who told King David, "Your house and your kingdom shall endure before Me forever; your throne shall be established forever" (2 Sam. 7:16, NASB).

14 "Just as Moses lifted up the snake in the wilderness, so the Son of Man must be lifted up," 15 "that everyone who believes may have eternal life in him."

God desires to be worshiped alone and commanded the Israelites, "Do not worship any other god" (Exod. 34:14). Furthermore God's instructions were clear as described in the second of the 10 commandments "You shall not make for yourself an image in the form of anything in heaven above or on the earth beneath or in the waters below. You shall not bow down to them or worship them" (Deut. 5:8–9). The reason for this can be understood through the name and nature of God as shown in the following passage, "The Lord, whose name is Jealous, is a jealous God" (Exod. 34:14). Why is God a jealous God? The reason for God's jealousy is his love for each and every one of us as God does not want "anyone to perish, but everyone to come to repentance" (2 Pet. 3–9). Thus, instead of being "thrown into the lake of fire" (Rev. 20:14, NASB), as punishment for our sins, God wants us to experience *eternal life in him*, by believing and following him, the one and only true and living God.

In disobedience, there were many incidents of idol worship by the Israelites when they strayed and worshiped false gods like Asherah and Baal. In one specific incident, the Israelites became impatient while Moses was receiving the Law on top of Mount Sinai, and they not only turned to idolatry, but even cast a golden calf and started worshiping it as their God. Because of their sin, the people were punished severely for their idolatry. In lieu of the story of the Golden Calf and the nature of God, it must have been very confusing, when some time later while still wandering in the wilderness, God told the Israelites to "make a snake and put it up on a pole" (Num. 21:8). (I described my confusion on this same point as well in chapter 4 Understanding What Is Truth but as I described, this passage of scripture was powerfully revealed to me).

It was a time when the Israelites were in rebellion to God, specifically they were rejecting God's free gift of *manna from heaven* and proclaimed that "we detest this miserable food!" (Num. 21:5). God's punishment of the Israelite's sins was poisonous snakes, which bit the Israelites, causing death. Following God's instructions, the Israelites made a bronze snake and put it on a pole, and once bitten, they were further instructed to seek out the *bronze snake* which was placed up on a pole and to "look at it and live" (Num. 21:8).

While perplexing in the past and throughout ancient history, the story of the *bronze snake* can be clearly explained now through understanding the design of history focused on Christ. *Just as Moses lifted up the snake in the desert so the Son of Man must be lifted up* refers to Jesus being *lifted up* on a pole, which was in the form of a cross

75

after he was crucified. Additionally, once bitten, the Israelites would go and search out the *bronze snake* on the pole to be prevented from physical death. In an analogous way, all of us today carry around the stench of sin, but for those who seek out Jesus, their sins will be forgiven like the removal of the snake's poison. Moreover, rather than being saved from physical death of the body as with the bronze snake, seeking out Christ will result in being saved from eternal death resulting in everlasting life (i.e., salvation).

16 For God so loved the world that he gave his one and only Son, "that whoever believes in him shall not perish but have eternal life."

God told Abraham, when he was old that he will be "the father of many nations" (Gen. 17:4), and even though he and his wife Sarah were well beyond the age of child bearing, through a miracle they had a son named Isaac. When Isaac was a young man, God told Abraham to "take now your son, your only son, whom you love, Isaac, and go to the land of Moriah, and offer him there as a burnt offering on one of the mountains of which I will tell you" (Gen. 22:2, NASB). After making preparations for the sacrifice, Abraham obediently bound his son and almost certainly would have been in the process of placing the knife at his son's neck to sacrifice him. However, at this last moment, God sent an angel and stopped him and then provided a ram for the sacrifice. The location where this occurred was on top of Mount Moriah, which would later become also the location of both the first and second Jewish Temples.

This story of Abraham and his son, Isaac, and the sacrifice that almost happened is one that must have puzzled the Israelites for generations. Human sacrifice including killing of babies was common among the Canaanite tribes. However, God specifically and clearly instructed the Israelites that this was forbidden in the following passages of the Law from Scripture, "Let no one be found among you who sacrifices their son or daughter in the fire" (Deut. 18:10), and "anyone who does these things is detestable to the Lord; because of these same detestable practices the Lord your God will drive out those nations before you" (Deut. 18:12).

However, now through revelation of Scripture, the meaning and reason for this event, which occurred over two thousand years before Christ was born, can be understood. Abraham was told to sacrifice *your son, your only son, whom you love.* In John 3:16, *His one and only son* clearly refers to Jesus Christ, whom God dearly loves. God the Father stated this, for example, at the time of Jesus's baptism by John, when he said "This is my son, whom I love; with him I am well pleased" (Matt. 3:17). Furthermore, because Abraham was faithful and was willing to sacrifice his son, Abraham was promised to be the father of many nations, and all nations would be blessed through him. God's son, Jesus Christ, would be sacrificed and would die on the cross. Through the sacrifice of God's son, Jesus Christ, all people of all nations were blessed, and a pathway for salvation was established.

17 "For God did not send his Son into the world to condemn the world, but to save the world through him."

Joseph, after being sold into slavery by his brothers, was then blessed by God to become second in power to Pharaoh in Egypt. This event resulted in Abrahams's line through Isaac, Jacob, and Jacob's sons, who would become the twelve tribes of Israel being saved by moving to Egypt after famine had decimated the land of Canaan. The Israelites were originally welcomed and protected in Egypt but after Joseph's death, they became slaves to the Egyptians. Removal from slavery proved to be very difficult for the Israelites and they were enslaved for over four hundred years. Moses was raised up by God to be the redeemer of the people of Israel and take them out of slavery to the Promised Land. Nine successive plagues, all very harsh, brought on by God through Moses, did not convince Pharaoh to let God's people go. It was only the tenth plague, the death of the firstborn, which finally resulted in the Israelite people being removed from slavery.

In order to be protected by God, the Israelites were instructed to sacrifice an unblemished male lamb (or goat). The lamb needed to be killed and then its blood had to be sprinkled around the doorpost of each home. As taught in Scripture, "The life of a creature is in the blood" and the sprinkling of the blood represented atonement as "it is the blood that makes atonement for one's life" (Lev. 17:11). When the death angel was released, any house that had the blood of the Passover lamb was spared but the firstborn of each household without the protection of the blood was killed. Scripture records that when the death angel was released that "there was loud wailing in Egypt, for there was not a house without someone dead" (Exod. 12:30). The Israelites obeying the Lord and being protected from death during the Passover, followed by their removal from slavery, are the most singular events of the Old Testament. However, without the context of Christ, the meaning of these events, occurring over 1300 years before Jesus was born, are not clear and must have puzzled the ancient scholars.

Now the meaning of these events can be understood through Christ. Today, we are all still slaves, not slaves in Egypt, but instead we are all slaves to sin. In an analogous way, like the Israelites who were mired in slavery for centuries before their redeemer Moses, we are mired in the slavery of sin, which is very difficult to remove in our lives (in fact impossible) without our redeemer, who is Christ. The Passover of the Israelites by the death angel used the blood from an unblemished lamb. Jesus Christ was the perfect sacrifice as he was unblemished by living a sinless life and became like the Passover lamb. When describing Jesus's death on the cross, the Apostle Paul wrote, "For Christ, our Passover lamb, has been sacrificed" (1 Cor. 5:7). Thus, God *saved the world* through the blood of Christ, and while Christ's blood was shed at enormous cost, this allows us to be *passed over* during the future time of judgment. Jesus's sacrificial death also provides a pathway for us to be removed from our slavery and to be brought to the *Promised Land,* which is heaven.

18 "Whoever believes in him is not condemned, but whoever does not believe stands condemned already because they have not believed in the name of God's one and only Son."

God created the heavens and the earth during the first six days, and upon completion saw all that he had made and said that "it was very good" (Gen. 1:31). At this point in history, sin and death had

not entered the world. It was only when Satan, in the form of a serpent, tempted Adam and Eve that they could "be like God" (Gen.
3:5, NASB), that they ate of the forbidden fruit and sin entered the
world and ruined God's perfect creation. After the fall of mankind,
God told Adam, "Cursed is the ground because of you" (Gen. 3:17,
NASB). At this moment, Adam and Eve were, for the first, time
ashamed of their nakedness, and shortly afterward, death entered the
world when God covered them with animal skins. This was the first
indication that sin would need to be paid with death and with blood.

With the establishment of the Tabernacle and later the Temple,
a system of animal sacrifice in order to make atonement for or to
cover the sins of the people was established. The High Priest was
appointed "to represent the people in matters related to God, to offer
gifts and sacrifices for sins" (Heb. 5:1). Each year during the Day of
Atonement, the High Priest would "offer sacrifices for his own sins,
as well as for the sins of the people." (Heb. 5:3). He would pray for
all of their sins to be transferred to an animal, which was then sacrificed and killed. As the people would continue sinning, animals
would have to be sacrificed repeatedly to cover the sins of the people.
Thus, the seriousness of sin as viewed by God is clearly shown by the
requirement to kill animals and take their life to atone or cover our
sins. Like the ancient Israelites, our sins condemn us today.

Stands condemned already means that the default condition in
our lives is we are sinful beings and are thus condemned. Scripture
clearly states that "all have sinned and fall short of the glory of God"
(Rom. 3:23, NASB). Thus, when we are born, we are born into sin
and during our lives we are all sinners. "Sin entered the world through
one man (Adam), and death through sin, and in this way death came
to all people, because all sinned" (Rom. 5:12). The sin chain, which
was continually passed down each generation from father to son,
was then broken through Jesus since he was not conceived by man
but was fathered through the Holy Spirit, lived his life without sin,
and died with uncorrupted flesh. Thus, the sin line was broken from
Adam to Jesus "for just as through the disobedience of the one man
the many were made sinners, so also through the obedience of the
one man the many will be made righteous" (Rom. 5:19). Through

Jesus, "God made him who had no sin to be sin for us, so that in him we might become the righteousness of God" (2 Cor. 5:21).

To be *not condemned* points directly to our need for a savior, which is *God's one and only Son* who is Jesus Christ. Without the forgiving of our sins, we would die in our sins because "the wages of sin is death" (Rom. 6:23, NASB), Jesus was designated by God to be "a merciful and faithful high priest in service to God, and that he might make atonement for the sins of the people" (Heb. 2:17). Through his sacrifice on the cross and the shedding of his blood, Jesus "having been made perfect, He became to all those who obey Him the source of eternal salvation" (Heb. 5:9, NASB). Instead of sins only being covered by the blood of the animals which needs to be repeated, Jesus's perfect sacrifice removed the stain of sin, once and for all, "For by one sacrifice he has made perfect forever those who are being made holy" (Heb. 10:14).

Chapter 7

Understanding Who Killed Jesus

As discussed in the previous chapter, the most seminal moment in all of history was Jesus Christ dying on the cross. A common question related to this pivotal event is *who* killed Jesus? The context of this question seems to infer the general thought that Jesus's ministry was cut prematurely short as he was only about thirty-three when he was crucified. Different viewpoints on who killed Jesus can be broken up into seven different lines of thought:

1) It was the Jewish religious leaders in the Sanhedrin (i.e., the ruling council) who killed Jesus. The religious leaders in particular were false witnesses and brought up "malicious accusations" (Ps. 27:12) against Jesus to the Roman Governor Pontius Pilate including that Jesus was a revolutionary, that he wanted to challenge Caesar as king, and that he wanted to "destroy the temple of God" (Matt. 26:61).

2) It was Caiaphas, the Jewish high priest who killed Jesus. Caiaphas, while at his palace, was the leader who assembled the Sanhedrin and put together the scheme "to arrest Jesus secretly and kill him" (Matt. 26:4). Once captured, Jesus was then able to be crucified by the Roman authorities.

3) It was the Jewish people, who killed Jesus, consistent with their ancestors who also "killed the prophets" (Luke 11:48). During the time of the Passover, the people had the

opportunity to have Jesus released when Pilate gave them a choice of letting one prisoner free but instead of choosing Jesus to set free, they choose instead Barabbas, a revolutionary. This choice ultimately sealed Jesus's fate.

4) It was Pilate who killed Jesus. Pilate, as the Roman governor, had the authority to have prisoners put to death. Pilate initially tried to set Jesus free, but eventually ordered "Jesus flogged, and handed him over to be crucified" (Matt. 27:26). Pilate gave this order even though he knew Jesus was an innocent man, and in spite of Pilate washing his hands in water and declaring that he was "innocent of this man's blood" (Matt. 27:24).

5) It was the Roman soldiers who killed Jesus. The soldiers did not just follow orders, but instead maliciously treated and abused Jesus. They "twisted together a crown of thorns and set it on his head," "mocked him," "spit on him," and "took the staff and struck him on the head again and again" (Matt. 27:29–30). Finally, after all of this humiliation, they carried out orders and crucified Jesus by nailing him to the cross, which directly led to his death.

6) It was Judas Iscariot who killed Jesus. Judas after being paid "30 pieces of silver" (Matt. 26:15), directed the soldiers to the remote area on the Mount of Olives, where Jesus could be captured without interference from the people. Furthermore, Judas betrayed Jesus "with a kiss" (Luke 22:48, NASB), thus positively identifying Jesus to the Roman guards, which lead to his capture.

7) It was Satan who killed Jesus. Satan "entered Judas" (Luke 22:3) prior to Judas going to the Sanhedrin to discuss how Jesus might be betrayed. Additionally, Satan, almost certainly, would have had great influence in stirring up the crowds against Jesus. The people's change in attitude was sudden and surprising, as only a few days earlier, they had hailed Jesus crying out "Blessed is the king of Israel!" (John 12:13) when he entered Jerusalem.

While all of these viewpoints are different, a characteristic feature of all of these views is that they are all only plausible if one denies the true deity of Christ as God. These also have a commonality in beliefs that God's plan from ancient times could be altered or thwarted. It is important to note that before Jesus could be crucified, he had to be first be captured. Thus, *who killed Jesus* can be understood by examining Scripture in detail by focusing on the capture of Jesus in the Garden of Gethsemane on the Mount of Olives.

Key details in the capture of Jesus started with Judas Iscariot being paid "30 pieces of silver" (Matt. 26:15) in order to betray Jesus. Judas led a "large crowd armed with swords and clubs" (Matt. 26:47), which included "a detachment of soldiers and some officials from the chief priests and the Pharisees" (John 18:3). Jesus, knowing all that was going to happen to him, went out and asked them, "Who is it you want?' 'Jesus of Nazareth,' they replied. 'I am he,' Jesus said. (And Judas the traitor was standing there with them). When Jesus said, 'I am he,' they drew back and fell to the ground" (John 18:4–6).

Later, as the men stepped forward, Peter, one of Jesus's disciples, drew a sword and "struck the servant of the high priest, cutting off his ear" (Matt. 26:51). Jesus told Peter to "put your sword back in its place." (Matt. 26:52). Jesus then "touched the man's ear and healed him" (Luke 22:51). Jesus said to his disciples, "Do you think I cannot call on my Father, and he will at once put at my disposal more than twelve legions of angels? But how then would the Scriptures be fulfilled that say it must happen in this way?" (Matt. 26:53–54).

Jesus addressed the soldiers and officials and said, "Am I leading a rebellion, that you have come out with swords and clubs to capture me? Every day I sat in the temple courts teaching, and you did not arrest me. But this has all taken place that the writings of the prophets might be fulfilled" (Matt. 26:55–56). Jesus then told them, "But this is your hour—when darkness reigns" (Luke 22:53).

After examining these verses, it appears that Jesus let himself be captured. Even more insight on what really happened can be gained by examining what Jesus said during his capture and this will reveal whether Jesus was really overpowered or instead if he was really in control during the entire time of his capture;

1) "Who is it you want?" (John 18:4).

The very evening of his capture, before crossing the Kidron Valley and entering the olive grove called the Garden of Gethsemane, Jesus predicted his death during the Passover dinner with his disciples which has been known since as *The Last Supper*. What Jesus said to his disciples was recorded in the following verses, "I have earnestly desired to eat this Passover with you before I suffer; for I say to you, I shall never again eat it until it is fulfilled in the kingdom of God.' And when He had taken a cup and given thanks, He said, 'Take this and share it among yourselves; for I say to you, I will not drink of the fruit of the vine from now on until the kingdom of God comes" (Luke 22:15–19, NASB). Later after traveling to the Garden of Gethsemane, Jesus fell with "his face to the ground and prayed, 'My Father, if it is possible, may this cup be taken from me. Yet not as I will, but as you will'" (Matt. 26:39). Thus, it is clear from these recorded incidents that Jesus knew well before the armed crowd arrived that he would be captured and killed. While having plenty of time to escape, Jesus did nothing to evade capture. When the armed crowd came, even before uttering, *Who is it you want?* (John 18:4), Jesus had already known "all that was going to happen to him" (John 18:4).

2) "I am he" (John 18:5).

The "large crowd armed with swords and clubs" (Matt. 26:47), which included "a detachment of soldiers and some officials from the chief priests and the Pharisees" (John 18:3), was not an unstoppable force, at least not one when confronting God, the creator of the universe. As was discussed earlier, God told Moses from the burning bush that his name is "I am who I am and to tell the Israelites that "I am has sent me to you." (Exod. 3:14). Thus, when Jesus said *I am he*, Jesus was declaring himself with authority and power, not as a man, but as God. Faced with this overwhelming power from a mere simple statement from God, the armed mob did not rush forward but instead "drew back and fell to the ground." (John 18:4–6). In no way, then was this armed mob in control of the situation but it was Jesus who was firmly in control.

3) "Put your sword back in its place" (Matt. 26:52).

After the armed mob got up off the ground and finally moved in to capture the unresisting Jesus, Peter drew his sword and drew the first blood and "struck the servant of the high priest, cutting off his ear." A clear act of rebellion, this powerful blow just missed its mark by the untrained hand of Peter. The ear is a very sensitive piece of anatomy and when cut off must have been very painful with the release of a lot of blood. Thus, this act could have quickly led to a fight and many deaths. However, rather than resisting, Jesus immediately ended all rebellion by ordering Peter to "put your sword back in its place" (Matt. 26:52). Furthermore, Jesus quickly asserted control over this situation again by miraculously healing the ear of the servant of the high priest. This must have been a startling sight to behold, which would have shaken further the already stunned armed mob.

4) "Do you think I cannot call on my Father, and he will at once put at my disposal more than twelve legions of angels" (Matt. 26:53).

A Roman legion during the time of Christ was about five thousand men and Jesus said that he could have "at once put at my disposal more than twelve legions of angels." (Matt. 26:53). Jesus was clearly declaring the nature of the overwhelming superior force that he could command and bring instantly to bear to fight for him. Angels are created beings, which were made to serve God and have enormous power. How powerful are angels? During the siege of Jerusalem, when Hezekiah was king, after he and the people repented of their sins, in one "night the angel of the LORD went out and put to death a 185,000 men in the Assyrian camp" (2 Kings 19:35). These were all heavily armed, battle hardened, Assyrian warriors and all were killed by a single angel in one night. Thus, if Jesus had instantly released the power and might of possibly sixty thousand angels, this would have been no contest and the armed mob including the soldiers and officials would have been overwhelmed and neutralized instantly.

5) "But this has all taken place that the writings of the prophets might be fulfilled" (Matt. 26:56).

As was discussed in chapter 6 (Understanding History's Design), all events from the creation of the world were leading up to God's plan of sending his son to die on the cross for the forgiveness of the sins of mankind. Thus, the plan for salvation was on track, and unstoppable from the beginning. Right after the fall of mankind, which may have been Satan's greatest moment, the ultimate victory that Christ would fulfill was predicted. God told the serpent, which was Satan, that the woman's seed "will crush your head, and you will strike his heel" (Gen. 3:15). Jesus's death on the cross seemed like a great victory for Satan as he did not understand God's plan. However, through Jesus's sacrifice (i.e., a strike on the heel), Jesus overcame sin and death, and gained a great victory over Satan (i.e., crushed his head) as predicted.

The question then remains who did kill Jesus? It should be clear at this point that Jesus is God and no one or any group of any size could have overpowered or killed Jesus. Thus, with this understanding, it should be clear that the seven viewpoints presented earlier could not have caused Jesus's death. Additionally, our sin did not kill Jesus because our sin results in our own personal damnation and has no power over God. Jesus provided the answer to this question when he said, "The reason my Father loves me is that I lay down my life —only to take it up again. No one takes it from me, but I lay it down of my own accord. I have authority to lay it down and authority to take it up again. This command I received from my Father" (John 10:17–18). Thus, no one killed Jesus but instead Jesus, obeying the will of the Father, laid down his life for us. Jesus willingly paid the ultimate penalty, out of his love for humanity and love for each of us individually, with the desire that no one should perish and be cast into hell. The clear reason for Jesus's death and sacrifice can be best summed up in the following verses,

> "For God so loved the world that he gave his one and only Son, that whoever believes in him shall not perish but have eternal life. For God did not send his Son into the world to condemn the world, but to save the world through him" (John 3:16–17).

Chapter 8

Understanding Who Is
the Living God?

Everyone, whether they admit it or not, serves a god (i.e., lowercase g which signifies a false god), which for them personally may be a multitude of things. Unfortunately for many, god represents money, which can be in many forms, currency, precious metals, and/or retirement accounts (IRA's, 401K etc.). For others, god may represent personal glory, which may manifest itself as a championship\trophy, an Olympic medal, another rung up the office ladder, achieving a managerial position, or becoming president and CEO. Nevertheless, the question remains, *who* is the *living god?* Note, a thorough description of God is beyond the scope of this book and quite frankly well above and beyond the scope of any book, which can ever be written by anyone.

What God is *not*, is quite clear. God is not an idol of wood, stone, ceramic, metal, or anything else that can be made by human hands. Making an idol is a form of idolatry, and Scripture teaches clearly against this in the following passage, "Cursed is the man who makes an idol or a molten image, an abomination to the Lord" (Deut. 27:15, NASB). What is God then? In one sentence, God is a living being who is infinite and exists everywhere at all times, is an almighty ruler in complete control of all things in his creation, and has unlimited knowledge, understanding everything. In summary, God is an immeasurable awesome being with enormous unlimited power.

How powerful is God? Starting with nothing, God "created the heavens and the earth" (Gen. 1:1, NASB). With just words, God spoke and said, "Let there be light'; and there was light" (Gen. 1:3, NASB). On a clear night, one can look to the stars where the "heavens declare the glory of God; the skies proclaim the work of his hands" (Ps. 19:1).

How big is the universe? Scientists have recently estimated from reviewing data from the NASA's Hubble Space Telescope that the universe includes two trillion galaxies (Hubblesite News). Furthermore, each galaxy may contain hundreds of billions of stars. Our own Milky Way galaxy, for example, contains an estimated one to four hundred billion stars (Howell 2014). Thus, God's creation is beyond immense, almost limitless, and well-beyond human imagination. The prophet Jeremiah affirms Gods' power, when in great distress from the Babylonian's siege of Jerusalem, he prayed to God and said, "You have made the heavens and the earth by Your great power and by Your outstretched arm! Nothing is too difficult for You" (Jer. 32:17, NASB). God answered and affirmed Jeremiah's words and said, "Behold, I am the Lord, the God of all flesh; is anything too difficult for Me?" (Jer. 32:27, NASB).

God describes himself through the prophet Isaiah in the following passage,

> "I am God, and there is no other; I am God, and there is no one like Me, Declaring the end from the beginning, And from ancient times things which have not been done, Saying, 'My purpose will be established, And I will accomplish all My good pleasure'; Calling a bird of prey from the east, The man of My purpose from a far country. Truly I have spoken; truly I will bring it to pass. I have planned it, surely I will do it" (Isa. 46: 9–11, NASB).

In addition to the stars, a prominent testimony for God is provided and present in all his creation, "For since the creation of the world His invisible attributes, His eternal power and divine nature, have been clearly seen, being understood through what has been made" (Rom. 1:20, NASB) and the "whole earth is full of His glory" (Isa. 6:3, NASB).

What additional characteristics does God exhibit? Foremost of all, God is a holy being as Scripture records that "There is no one holy like the Lord" (1 Sam. 2:2, NASB), and God definitively said about himself "I the Lord your God am holy" (Lev. 19:2, NASB). Scripture records that God "loves righteousness and justice" (Ps. 33:5, NASB), that God is "rich in mercy, because of His great love with which He loved us" (Eph. 2:4, NASB), and that "God is love" (1 John 4:8, NASB).

Furthermore, God's "love is better than life" (Ps. 63:3), and that God's love has been "lavished on us, that we should be called children of God!" (1 John 3:1). With respect to character Scripture records that God is "a gracious and compassionate God, slow to anger and abundant in lovingkindness, and one who relents concerning calamity" (Jon. 4:2, NASB). Additionally, God himself emphatically declares that "I am the Lord who exercises lovingkindness, justice and righteousness on earth; for I delight in these things" (Jer. 9:24, NASB). While unlimited in ability, Scripture records that God "remains faithful, for He cannot deny Himself" (2 Tim. 2:13, NASB), that "it is impossible for God to lie" (Heb. 6:18, NASB), and that with God "there is no variation" (James 1:17, NASB). Furthermore, God definitively says about himself, "I, the Lord, do not change" (Mal. 3:6, NASB).

As described earlier, God's glory and power and wisdom and knowledge is unimaginable and unfathomable by human minds. When Moses asked God what his name was, God replied, "I AM WHO I AM," and God told Moses to tell his fellow Israelites, "I AM has sent me to you" (Exod. 3:14). God also said to Moses to tell the Israelites to identify him throughout all future generations as "the God of Abraham, the God of Isaac, and the God of Jacob" (Exod. 3:15). Additional information about God and his make-up was revealed during the time of the creation of the world. It was on the sixth day when God said, "Let Us make man in Our image, according to Our likeness" (Gen. 1:26, NASB). In this passage, God said

Our image and *Our likeness* (i.e., plural), not my image and my likeness (i.e., singular). This usage of the term *Us* must have puzzled the ancient Israelites as God's identity was not yet fully revealed. From studying the full revelation of Scripture in the Old and the New Testament, it is clear that *Us* refers to the plural nature of God. God exists as one being, but in three separate personages, who are God the Father, God the Son, who is Jesus, and the Holy Spirit. Thus, God exists as a plural being, which has been described by mankind as the Trinity, which means three in one.

Understanding the Trinity is extremely difficult since we are singular and not plural beings. Perhaps, three distinct parts contained in one can be understood, at least partly by analogy. An everyday example would be the egg, which while being one item, is made up on a macroscale of three distinct parts (i.e., shell, egg white, and yolk) with different complementary functions; the shell is hard and protective but permeable to air, the white is protective of the embryo and provides protein, and the yolk is sacrificial and provides food especially fat for the development and growth of the embryo to become a chick.

A molecular example would be water at its triple point (273 K at 612 Pascal), which is a unique condition whereby all three phases including steam, water, and ice coexist simultaneously. Each phase of water exhibits uniquely distinct physical characteristics; steam being a gas, water being a liquid, and ice being a solid. The basic building block of matter is broken down into discrete units called atoms. A simple model of the atom shows three main constituent parts with neutral neutrons and positive protons existing in the nucleus and negatively charged electrons existing in discrete energy levels or shells outside of the nucleus. As noted earlier, all of these analogies fall way short of describing the complexity and glory of God, but may help a little bit in this understanding of his make-up of three personages in one being.

While the word Trinity is not mentioned in Scripture, there are numerous scriptural verses, which describe the three separate personages of God in one passage. For example, when John the Baptist baptized Jesus in the Jordan River, the incident was recorded in Scripture (with the identity clarified in brackets), "At that moment heaven was opened, and he (i.e., Jesus Christ) saw the Spirit of God (i.e., Holy Spirit) descending like a dove and alighting on him (i.e., Jesus Christ). And a voice from heaven (i.e., God the Father) said, "This is my Son (i.e., Jesus Christ), whom I (i.e., God the Father) love; with him (i.e., Jesus Christ) I (i.e., God the Father) am well pleased" (Matt. 3:16–17). Another example occurred after the resurrection of Jesus and just prior to Jesus being taken up in a cloud on the Mount of Olives. Jesus speaking to his disciples said, "All authority has been given to Me in heaven and on earth. Go therefore and make disciples of all the nations, baptizing them in the name of the Father and the Son and the Holy Spirit, teaching them to observe all that I commanded you" (Matt. 28:18–20, NASB).

In spite of our limited understanding of the Trinity, Scripture does reveal different roles of the three personages of God. An example is when Jesus told the disciples prior to his death (with the identity clarified in brackets), "When the Advocate (i.e., Holy Spirit) comes, whom I (Jesus) will send to you from the Father (i.e., God the Father)—the Spirit of truth (i.e., Holy Spirit) who goes out from the Father (i.e., God the Father)—he (i.e., Holy Spirit) will testify about me (i.e., Jesus)" (John 15:26).

Another example describes God's elect (i.e., saved believers) as those, "who have been chosen according to the foreknowledge of God the Father, through the sanctifying work of the Spirit, to be obedient to Jesus Christ and sprinkled with his blood" (1 Pet. 1:2). Thus, it is apparent that God the Father is the director of all events and knowledge and represents the guiding leader. The Holy Spirit is sent as a helper to provide "power from on high" (Luke 24:49, NASB) and to convict people of their sin so that they will seek repentance. Jesus, the Son, was sent to the earth to become a man, live a sinless life, and die for our sins on the cross. Jesus is also the "one mediator between God and mankind" (1 Tim. 2:5), and in the future will be the intercessor between us and God the Father.

While we cannot fully understand God, we can develop a personal relationship with God as "God created man in His own image" (Gen. 1:27, NASB). Once accepting Christ, a personal relationship is forged since you will be filled with the Holy Spirit. When the "Spirit of truth, comes, He will guide you into all the truth; for He will not speak on His own initiative, but whatever He hears, He will speak; and He will disclose to you what is to come" (John 16:13, NASB). In chapter 4 (Understanding What Is Truth), it was discussed how the Holy Spirit reveals the truth of Scripture. Jesus declared, "In fact, the reason I was born and came into the world is to testify to the truth" (John 18:37). We, as humans, can relate to Jesus easier since Jesus came on the earth as a man and interacted directly with us. Furthermore, scripture reveals a lot more about Jesus than the other personages of God. Thus, to understand further *Who is the Living God*, involves understanding *Who is Jesus*, which is the focus of the next chapter.

Chapter 9

Understanding Who Is Jesus?

The term 'god' has become rather benign in modern culture, and sometimes it seems that everyone has their own god. For some, it is very easy to talk about their own personal god because they may have molded it from their own image, and it is themselves. However, it can be much more difficult to talk about Jesus (i.e., the true and living God) as the name of Jesus is often what inflames and causes an immediate reaction. Often these reactions are diverse and can be polar opposite even in the same set of circumstances. For example, during Jesus's crucifixion, there were "women who mourned and wailed for him" (Luke 23:27), while others "passing by were hurling abuse at Him" including the chief priests and the scribes who "were mocking Him" (Mark 15:29–30). In a similar fashion, consider the individual responses of the two thieves on the cross. "One of the criminals who hung there hurled insults at him: 'Aren't you the Messiah? Save yourself and us!' But the other criminal rebuked him. 'Don't you fear God,' he said, 'since you are under the same sentence?'" (Luke 23:39–40). Moreover, the very name of Jesus or Jesus Christ has become a swear word for many, which is uttered in anger or disgust. Taking the Lord's name in vain, whether it is realized or not, is a very serious business as God is a holy God. Scripture specifically forbids this and says, "You shall not swear falsely by My name, so as to profane the name of your God; I am the Lord" (Lev. 19:12, NASB).

It should be quite interesting, whether you are a believer or not, why the name of Jesus involves such strong feelings two thousand years after his death. Understanding this, involves understanding *Who is Jesus?* From a historical perspective, Jesus was a man that lived in the land of Israel about two thousand years ago. In spite of what you may have heard, this is not open for debate but is a well-established fact. In addition to the extensive Biblical history recorded about Jesus's birth, life, death, and resurrection, there are several other historical works, which were written about Jesus by independent sources. For example, Publius Tacitus was a senator and Roman historian and wrote about the history of the Roman Empire. Tacitus recorded the following around 116 AD, "Nero fastened the guilt and inflicted the most exquisite tortures on a class hated for their abominations, called Christians by the populous. Christus from whom the name had its origin, suffered the extreme penalty during the reign of Tiberias at the hands of one of our procurators, Pontius Pilate, and a most mischievous superstition, thus checked for the moment, again broke out not only in Judea, the first source of the evil, but even in Rome" (Tacitus).

Another example is the writing of Josephus Flavius, a Jewish historian. In 93 AD, Josephus refers to Jesus in the following passage, "Now there was about this time Jesus, a wise man, if it be lawful to call him a man; for he was a doer of wonderful works, a teacher of such men as receive the truth with pleasure. He drew over to him both many of the Jews and many of the Gentiles. He was (the) Christ; And when Pilate, at the suggestion of the principal men amongst us, had condemned him to the cross, those that loved him at the first did not forsake him; for he appeared to them alive again the third day; as the divine prophets had foretold these and ten thousand other wonderful things concerning him; And the tribe of Christians, so named from him, are not extinct at this day" (The Works of Josephus). Interestingly, Josephus, also mentioned John the Baptist (the forerunner to Christ and a voice in the wilderness) in his writings in the following passage, "John, that was called the Baptist for Herod slew him, who was a good man and commanded the Jews to exercise virtue; both as to righteousness towards one another and piety towards God, and so to come to baptism" (The Works of Josephus).

Now that it is established that Jesus is a historical figure, the next question then is who or what was Jesus? Many people (non-believers) might say that Jesus was a good man, or that he was a prophet, or that he was a smart man, or one of the greats like others in the past. Others might say evil, dark, and blasphemous things about Jesus and further deny his deity. Regardless of what opinion one might have, Jesus certainly is the most talked about, most interesting, and most controversial man who has ever lived on this earth. There was a righteous old man named Simeon, who lived in Jerusalem during the time of Jesus and met Jesus firsthand. Upon seeing the baby Jesus, Simeon, filled by the Holy Spirit, said to Mary, his mother,

> "Behold, this Child is appointed for the fall and rise of many in Israel, and for a sign to be opposed— and a sword will pierce even your own soul—to the end that thoughts from many hearts may be revealed" (Luke 2:34–35, NASB).

Thus, Jesus is the dividing line and there can be no neutral ground with respect to Jesus, so it is important that you learn as much as possible about Jesus so that you can make the right choices about him. During his ministry, Jesus told his followers, "All men will hate you because of me" (Luke 21:17), and that "Whoever is not with me is against me" (Matt. 12:30). Ultimately, you will have to make your own personal decision; to be a follower of Jesus (i.e., a Christian) or be against him, which is the default condition of the world.

Jesus declared himself to be God many times and in many ways. For example, in the temple courts, the Jews asked, "Are you greater than our father Abraham? He died, and so did the prophets. Who do you think you are?" (John 8:53). Jesus answered, "Your father Abraham rejoiced to see My day, and he saw it and was glad." So the Jews said to Him, "You are not yet fifty years old, and have You seen Abraham?" Jesus said to them, "Truly, truly, I say to you, before Abraham was born, I am" (John 8:56–59, NASB). Note that the Jews picked up stones to stone him since Jesus appeared to have committed the sin of blasphemy by using the phrase, *I am,* as he was declaring himself to be God. Another example occurred while in

Caesarea Philippi, Jesus asked his disciples, "Who do people say that the Son of Man is?' And they said, 'Some say John the Baptist; and others, Elijah; but still others, Jeremiah, or one of the prophets.' He said to them,

> 'But who do you say that I am?' Simon Peter answered, 'You are the Christ, the Son of the living God.' And Jesus said to him, "Blessed are you, Simon Barjona, because flesh and blood did not reveal this to you, but My Father who is in heaven" (Matt. 16:15–17, NASB).

Thus, no matter what you think about Jesus, there can be no middle ground; either Jesus was a deranged madman *claiming to be God* or Jesus *is God*.

Jesus is described by Scripture as "the radiance of God's glory and the exact representation of his being, sustaining all things by his powerful word." Jesus is both our high priest and our king, and with his death and resurrection has consolidated these separate roles (as a priest king). Jesus, as our priest, was described way back in the days of Abraham (over two thousand years before Jesus's birth), in the following passage, "Without father or mother, without genealogy, without beginning of days or end of life, resembling the Son of God, he remains a priest forever" (Heb. 7:3). Jesus Christ as a high priest was further described by the Apostle Paul in the following passage, "For it was fitting for us to have such a high priest, holy, innocent, undefiled, separated from sinners and exalted above the heavens; who does not need daily, like those high priests, to offer up sacrifices, first for His own sins and then for the sins of the people, because this He did once for all when He offered up Himself" (Heb. 7:26–27, NASB).

Jesus was predicted as a future king, even before he was conceived. The Angel Gabriel told his mother Mary that

> "you will conceive and give birth to a son, and you are to call him Jesus. He will be great and will be called the Son of the Most High. The Lord

God will give him the throne of his father David,
and he will reign over Jacob's descendants forever;
his kingdom will never end" (Luke 1:31–33).

Zechariah, over five hundred years before Christ was born, prophesized that the ruler will also be the priest in the following passages, "He will build the temple of the Lord. Yes, it is He who will build the temple of the Lord, and He who will bear the honor and sit and rule on His throne. Thus, He will be a priest on His throne, and the counsel of peace will be between the two offices" (Zech. 6:12–13, NASB). In the next chapter, further information will be provided about *who is Jesus* with further focus and understanding of Jesus's special role as the Savior.

Chapter 10

Understanding Jesus as Your Savior

After getting off the bus during a tour of Jerusalem, a devout young Jewish man, about twenty-five years old, asked me a question about my faith. He said that he has been studying the Law since his youth, and even after much diligent and focused study, was now just beginning to understand the full ramifications of the Law. He said, "You Christians seem so free and believe and act that you are unbound by the law. I don't understand, how this can be?" After the initial surprise, I said that we are free in Christ, and we believe that Jesus came to fulfill the Law referring to the following passage, "Do not think that I came to abolish the Law or the Prophets; I did not come to abolish but to fulfill" (Matt. 5:17, NASB). I explained that the Jewish prophets described the coming of the Messiah or Savior for thousands of years, and we believe that Jesus is this Messiah. While the Law establishes a standard, it is one that that we could never meet and, as such, it exposes our sin and the need for the Savior. Jesus *fulfilled* the Law, by providing a pathway for salvation for all.

After talking with him for several minutes, it was clear that this young man knew Old Testament Scripture including the Law, along with its many ramifications and modern interpretations. However, he didn't know Jesus as God who is revealed in the following passages of New Testament Scripture,

"The Son is the image of the invisible God, the firstborn over all creation. For in him all things were created: things in heaven and on earth, visible and invisible, whether thrones or powers or rulers or authorities; all things have been created through him and for him. He is before all things, and in him all things hold together. And he is the head of the body, the church; he is the beginning and the firstborn from among the dead, so that in everything he might have the supremacy. For God was pleased to have all his fullness dwell in him, and through him to reconcile to himself all things, whether things on earth or things in heaven, by making peace through his blood, shed on the cross" (Col. 1:15–20).

The next sections reveal more detail on how Jesus uniquely fulfilled the Law, through his divine role as our personal Savior.

The True Vine

Jesus said, "**I am** the true vine, and my Father is the Gardener" (John 15:1).

If Jesus is the vine and God the Father is the gardener, one may ask then, how do we become part of this garden? That is, how do we become part of God's kingdom? From ancient times, the Israelites have been God's chosen people and a nation set apart to honor God. However, the plan for bringing salvation to the gentiles (i.e., all people who are not Jewish) was first mentioned in God's covenant with Abraham about 2000 BC where he says, "Through your offspring all nations on earth will be blessed" (Gen. 22:18). Bringing salvation to the Gentiles was further reaffirmed through the prophet Isaiah over seven hundred years BC in the following passage, "I will also make You a light of the nations So that My salvation may reach to the end of the earth" (Isa. 49:6, NASB).

As described in chapter 5 (Understanding the Biblical History of the Universe), the Israelites repeatedly rejected God throughout their history, often in a cyclical fashion of sin followed by a time of repentance and redemption. These transgressions were not enough for God to reject his people. However, the Israelites also rejected God's son, Jesus Christ, who was the very Messiah that they were seeking for thousands of years. Because of this final rejection, God brought salvation to the "Gentiles to make Israel envious" (Rom. 11:11). Experiencing salvation as a Gentile through a Jewish God seems at first strange. However, this is clearly described by the Apostle Paul in the following passage, "you, though a wild olive shoot, have been grafted in among the others and now share in the nourishing sap from the olive root" (Rom. 11:17). Thus, we are blessed tremendously to be grafted into God's kingdom through Jesus, the true vine.

Jesus said, "I am the vine; you are the branches. If you remain in me and I in you, you will bear much fruit; apart from me you can do nothing" (John 15:5). Thus, all achievements, which bear much fruit, such as those, which lead to salvation of those sinners who are lost, are enabled through Jesus Christ. Jesus said, "I have other sheep that are not of this sheep pen. I must bring them also. They too will listen to my voice, and there shall be one flock and one shepherd" (John 10:16). Thus, it is clear that we all can be part of God's kingdom and be nourished by the one and only *true vine*, who is Jesus Christ!

The Good Shepherd

Jesus said, "**I am** the good shepherd; I know my sheep and my sheep know me—just as the Father knows me and I know the Father—and I lay down my life for the sheep" (John 10:15).

The concept of a shepherd and sheep is one that God uses throughout Scripture. Sheep are animals that are worthy as they can provide meat for food and wool for clothing. However, sheep are not very intelligent and need to be led to water and to food in order to survive. Additionally, they need to be guarded as they are practically defenseless and need to be protected constantly from predators that would destroy them.

A *bad shepherd* is one that leaves his sheep at the first sign of danger. However, a *good shepherd* is one that loves his sheep, watches over them carefully, and will fight for them in their time of danger, even to his own death. A *good shepherd* typifies Jesus in the following passage, "He tends his flock like a shepherd: He gathers the lambs in his arms and carries them close to his heart" (Isa. 40:11). Jesus told the following parable, "What man among you, if he has a hundred sheep and has lost one of them, does not leave the ninety-nine in the open pasture and go after the one which is lost until he finds it? When he has found it, he lays it on his shoulders, rejoicing. And when he comes home, he calls together his friends and his neighbors, saying to them, 'Rejoice with me, for I have found my sheep which was lost!'" (Luke 15:4–6, NASB). Thus, Jesus doesn't just love his herd of sheep, he loves them all individually.

Through his loving protection, Jesus provides guidance and comfort for his sheep as described by the following passage, "The Lord is my shepherd, I shall not want. He makes me lie down in green pastures; He leads me beside quiet waters. He restores my soul; He guides me in the paths of righteousness" (Pss. 23:1–3, NASB). It is important to note that the sheep will find *green pastures* and *quiet waters* not because of being good sheep but because they are being led by a *good shepherd*. Jesus is the *good shepherd* and lays his life down for his sheep as stated in the following passage, "For the Lamb at the center of the throne will be their shepherd; he will lead them to springs of living water" (Rev. 7:17). Note that the *Lamb* is in reference to the Passover lamb, which was sacrificed and killed so that the death angel would pass over and spare the life of the firstborn. Follow the good shepherd, "Christ, our Passover lamb" (1 Cor. 5:7), and he will lead you to *springs of living water*, which unlike normal water which satisfies thirst for only a little while, *living water* is nourishment to the soul for all eternity.

The Gate

Jesus said, "**I am** the gate; whoever enters through me will be saved" (John 10:9).

Often, people (nonbelievers) say that there are many routes to heaven. One may ask, how do they know this, have they been to heaven before? Were they with God when he created the heavens and the earth? Do they know the way? We all know that to get to any destination, such as a friend's house, a favorite restaurant, or an airport involves following a path and a set of directions. If it is a new destination, if you do not follow the directions, but travel blindly, you may not find the place that you seek and will get lost. Another example where following the exact directions is important is a password, such as that needed to turn on a computer or a cell phone. Even if you type the password mostly correctly, if you are just one character or one stroke off, then it will not unlock and you are not getting in. Now consider that heaven represents an extremely special destination, as it can only be reached after you have died and your soul has left your body. How your soul, without the body, finds heaven is clearly much more complex than the previous examples provided. Thus, one would surely think that a specific set of instructions would be needed to be followed exactly to get to heaven.

Let's examine what God, who made heaven, exists in heaven, and knows the way to heaven says about the place he made. Jesus said, "Enter through the narrow gate; for the gate is wide and the way is broad that leads to destruction, and there are many who enter through it. For the gate is small and the way is narrow that leads to life, and there are few who find it" (Matt. 7:13–14, NASB). Thus, there are only two paths for each of us after we die, and each path leads to two separate destinies. The wide gate leads to eternal destruction and damnation in the lake of fire or hell and is the place the majority will end up. Note that the wide gate is the default position since we are born with flesh and all of us live "gratifying the cravings of our flesh and following its desires and thoughts," and we are "by nature deserving of wrath" (Eph. 2:3). Only a few find the narrow gate and eternal life with God in heaven. The way to heaven is through the narrow gate since, to pass through this gate, you have to meet God's standard, which is perfection. Jesus is *the gate*, as only through his blood can you be cleansed, which then allows you to pass through to heaven and eternal life. Jesus said, "I came that they may have life, and have it abundantly" (John 10:10, NASB).

Is there truly any other way to heaven? In the Garden of Gethsemane, on the slope of the Mount of Olives, prior to his arrest by the armed guards, Jesus prayed earnestly to the Father to see if there was any way that sin could be removed rather than only through his own death. Jesus prayed, "My Father, if it is possible, may this cup be taken from me. Yet not as I will, but as you will" (Matt. 26:39). Note that the cup refers to the new covenant, which is the forgiveness of sins through Jesus's blood and sacrifice on the cross. Jesus prayed this prayer asking God the Father if there were any other way, not once but three different times with similar prayers. He prayed this so earnestly, knowing what faced him in the near future that "his sweat was like drops of blood falling to the ground" (Luke 22:44).

During the flogging and crucifixion, Jesus experienced unimaginable pain and utter humiliation as he was left naked and nailed to a cross and displayed for all to see in the city of Jerusalem. Isaiah prophesized about this very event over seven hundred years earlier in the following passage "there were many who were appalled at him— his appearance was so disfigured beyond that of any human being and his form marred beyond human likeness" (Isa. 52:14). If Jesus, who is God, could not find any other way than to be humiliated, beaten beyond recognition, and to die a horrible painful death on the cross, it is foolish to think that we can now discover another way or a new path for salvation in order to get to heaven.

The Way and the Truth and the Life

Jesus said, "**I am** the way and the truth and the life. No one comes to the Father except through me" (John 14:6).

Forgiveness of sins, which leads to *the life,* is accomplished through Jesus's death on the cross only. Jesus is *the way* and the only way to pay for the penalty for all sins, so that one may experience eternal life with the *Father* in heaven. If anyone tells you that Jesus plus "anything else" (i.e., *Jesus + X*) is needed for you to have your sins forgiven and achieve eternal life than the + *X* is wrong and is not *the truth.* Note that + *X* can come in a wide variety of added on stipulations such as being baptized into a particular church, performing good works, worshiping on a specific day, paying money for your sins, etc. During the time of Jesus, the religious leaders were focused on teaching the Law and all of the things that needed to be done in order to be right with God. Jesus while talking to them said, "You experts in the law, woe to you, because you load people down with burdens they can hardly carry, and you yourselves will not lift one finger to help them" (Luke 11:46). Furthermore, Jesus continued, "Woe to you experts in the law, because you have taken away the key to knowledge. You yourselves have not entered, and you have hindered those who were entering" (Luke 11:52).

One may ask if it really is that important to believe in Jesus only as *the way* to salvation? What harm could be done by adding the + *X* when acknowledging Jesus's sacrifice? The answer is the belief in anything that is a + *X*, places your entire salvation in doubt and is 100 percent vitally and profoundly important, to not add this to your beliefs. If you believe in *Jesus* + *X*, what you are really thinking is that Jesus's sacrifice for your sins was not quite good enough. You are denying in your heart, the sufficiency and adequacy of Jesus's death and sacrifice on the cross. This is the case, if Jesus is only part of your beliefs, or even if Jesus plays a significant major role in your beliefs. In order to be saved, you need to accept Jesus's death fully for your sins and realize that his payment was entirely sufficient and came at such a great cost, that it is only by grace that you are or any of us are saved, "For it is by grace you have been saved, through faith – and this not from yourselves" (Eph. 2:8). Jesus's sacrifice allows us the potential to escape from the enormous penalty, which we owe for our sins, which will result in eternal separation from God. How one can escape this penalty and be saved will be discussed in detail in chapter 16—Understanding How to Be Saved (Right Now).

The Resurrection and the Life

Jesus said, "**I am** the resurrection and the life. The one who believes in me will live, even though they die; and whoever lives by believing in me will never die" (John 11:25).

Death is the great equalizer, affecting young and old, rich, and poor, and the famous as well as the unknown. The majority of us fear death, albeit some of us greatly and some much less so. As we get older and feel our mortality to a greater extent, we generally want to delay the inevitable for as long as possible, which is death. However, should we live like this? Jesus, who would experience death, said, "Do not be afraid of those who kill the body and after that can do no more. But I will show you whom you should fear: Fear him who, after your body has been killed, has authority to throw you into hell" (Luke 12:4–5). Thus, we should not fear the first death but the second death.

The first death is rather straightforward and it involves the death of the body, which involves a separation of your soul from your body. You are born into this world, you live your life according to your free will, and then, at some point, you will die. Living in this world does not come with any guarantees, and some will die at birth, some will die while they are young, some will die in the prime of their lives, and a few others will die when they are old. What age you are when you die is not nearly as important as what condition you are in when you die as you will be sealed in this condition. Scripture teaches us that "people are destined to die once, and after that to face judgment" (Heb. 9:27). The second death occurs after you face judgment and are found guilty. The second death results in eternal separation of your soul from God, and is described specifically as being "thrown into the lake of fire" (Rev. 20:14, NASB), which represents eternal damnation.

The question then is how do you avoid the second death, which is the focus of Understanding Manna? The simple answer to this most important question is to be reborn. This concept of being reborn, or a second birth, was discussed by Jesus with a Pharisee named Nicodemus. Jesus declared, "'I tell you the truth, no one can see the kingdom of God unless he is born again.' Nicodemus asked 'How can a man be born again when he is old? Surely he cannot enter a second time into his mother's womb to be born!' Jesus answered, 'I tell you the truth, no one can enter the kingdom of God unless he is born of water and the Spirit. Flesh gives birth to flesh but the Spirit gives birth to spirit'" (John 3:3–6).

After you accept the gift of salvation from the blood of Jesus Christ, you are reborn with the Holy Spirit living within you. Through this second birth, you will gain victory over death. That is, victory over the only death that matters, which is the second death as the first death is only a natural part of life on this world. Your victory over death can then be shouted out,

> "'Where, O death, is your victory? Where, O death, is your sting?' The sting of death is sin, and the power of sin is the law. But thanks be to God! He gives us the victory through our Lord Jesus Christ" (1 Cor.15:55–57).

Chapter 11

Understanding Heaven and Hell

In the geography of the land of Israel, a type of heaven and a type of hell are provided in its boundaries with two great inland bodies of water—the Sea of Galilee and the Dead Sea. The Sea of Galilee is very inviting and teaming with life including several species of fish, birds of all kinds, crabs and shellfish, and even freshwater otters. The Dead Sea is foreboding and is amply named as the salinity contents are so high there is no life living there, only death. Analogous to these bodies of water, it is important to realize that heaven and hell are not just concepts but real places. If you visit Israel and had to pick which location to live, the choice would be easy. In an analogous fashion but to an infinitely greater extent, if you could choose your eternal destination (you can!), you would certainly choose to exist in heaven rather than hell.

Insight may be gained about heaven and hell in the following story/parable told by Jesus, "Now there was a rich man, and he habitually dressed in purple and fine linen, joyously living in splendor every day. And a poor man named Lazarus was laid at his gate, covered with sores, and longing to be fed with the crumbs which were falling from the rich man's table; besides, even the dogs were coming and licking his sores. Now the poor man died and was carried away by the angels to Abraham's bosom; and the rich man also died and was buried. In Hades he lifted up his eyes, being in torment, and saw Abraham far away and Lazarus in his bosom. And he cried out and said, Father Abraham, have mercy on me, and send Lazarus so that he may dip the tip of his finger in water and cool off my tongue, for I am in agony in this flame.' But Abraham said, 'Child, remember that during your life you received your good things, and likewise Lazarus bad things; but now he is being comforted here, and you are in agony. And besides all this, between us and you there is a great chasm fixed, so that those who wish to come over from here to you will not be able, and that none may cross over from there to us.' And he said, 'Then I beg you, father, that you send him to my father's house— for I have five brothers—in order that he may warn them, so that they will not also come to this place of torment.' But Abraham said, 'They have Moses and the Prophets; let them hear them.' But he said, 'No, father Abraham, but if someone goes to them from the dead, they will repent!' But he said to him, 'If they do not listen to Moses and the Prophets, they will not be persuaded even if someone rises from the dead'" (Luke 16:19–31, NASB).

In the previous passages, two distinct separate destinies are described for the rich man and Lazarus—the rich man went to a place of torment, and Lazarus went to a place of comfort. Note that biblical scholars are still debating the full ramifications of these passages, which seem to indicate the temporary heaven and temporary hell setup before the death and resurrection of Jesus. Nevertheless, it can be certainly ascertained that when you die you are powerfully and unchangeably sealed in your condition. The rich man clearly had not repented and, even though he was in a *place of torment*, he was still trying to order Lazarus around, even though Lazarus was now in a higher position. Furthermore, it is apparent that after you die, you are powerfully constrained and confined in your place of destination, so much that a *great chasm* is set up which is both uncrossable and inescapable. Finally, it is clear from the passages, that your eternal destiny is based on choices made while you are alive. After death, it is too late to repent of your sins and you will be judged for them as all "people are destined to die once, and after that to face judgment." (Heb. 9:27).

Hell is a place of indescribable torment, which is so bad that is must be avoided at all cost. Jesus, when describing hell, said the following, "If your hand causes you to stumble, cut it off; it is better for you to enter life crippled, than, having your two hands, to go into hell, into the unquenchable fire, (where their worm does not die, and the fire is not quenched). If your foot causes you to stumble, cut it off; it is better for you to enter life lame, than, having your two feet, to be cast into hell, (where their worm does not die, and the fire is not quenched). If your eye causes you to stumble, throw it out; it is better for you to enter the kingdom of God with one eye, than, having two eyes, to be cast into hell, where their worm does not die, and the fire is not quenched" (Mark 9:43–48, NASB).

Jesus, speaking about the unbelievers who are not saved at the end of the age, said he "will send out his angels and they will weed out of his kingdom everything that causes sin and all who do evil. They will throw them into the blazing furnace, where there will be weeping and gnashing of teeth" (Matt. 13:41–42). Jesus also describes this time of judgment as

> "like a dragnet cast into the sea, and gathering fish of every kind; and when it was filled, they drew it up on the beach; and they sat down and gathered the good fish into containers, but the bad they threw away. So it will be at the end of the age; the angels will come forth and take out the wicked from among the righteous, and will throw them into the furnace of fire; in that place there will be weeping and gnashing of teeth" (Matt. 13:47–50, NASB).

From these passages, it is clear that the wicked will be separated from the righteous. Furthermore, that no one enters hell willingly, but after being judged and convicted will be overpowered and *thrown into the blazing furnace,* which is hell.

There is no way to fully understand or comprehend what hell would be like. Hell is described as a "fiery lake of burning sulfur" (Rev. 19:20) and thus is a place of indescribable torment with "weeping and gnashing of teeth" (Matt. 13:41). As terrible as hell is, eternal separation from God and from all mankind would be by itself, a hell.

It is clear that God made man a social creature from the beginning and after making Adam "The LORD God said, 'It is not good for the man to be alone'" (Gen. 2:18), and then he made Eve. Prison is sometimes called a hell, and the worst part of prison has been described as solitary confinement, as for example, in the following quote, "The box is a place like no other place on planet Earth. It's a place where men full of rage can stand at their cell gates fulminating on their neighbor or neighbors, yelling and screaming and speaking some of the filthiest words that could ever come from a human mouth, do it for hours on end" (Blake 2013). Solitary confinement in prison appears to fit the description of *weeping and gnashing of teeth,* but as bad as this place is, it is certainly not even close to the magnitude of God's full punishment experienced in hell.

It is important to note that hell was not created for people, but Scripture records that hell was "prepared for the devil and his angels" (Matt. 25:41, NASB), and that God "wants all people to be saved and to come to a knowledge of the truth" (1 Tim. 2:4). Nevertheless, based on your own free will and choice, if you reject your Savior, you will be *thrown into hell.* If this occurs this means that you have been judged and found guilty, have been rejected by God, and will be eternally separated from your Creator forever. Alternatively, by accepting Jesus as your personal savior, you can be found innocent because you sins will be forgiven, and you can exist with God for eternity in heaven.

It is hard to understand what heaven will be like, and its glories are quite unimaginable. Jesus described heaven in the following examples, "The kingdom of heaven is like a treasure hidden in the field, which a man found and hid again; and from joy over it he goes and sells all that he has and buys that field. 'Again, the kingdom of heaven is like a merchant seeking fine pearls, and upon finding one pearl of great value, he went and sold all that he had and bought it'" (Matt. 13:44–46, NASB). Thus, while we still can't visualize what heaven would be like exactly, Jesus who came "down from heaven" (John 6:38, NASB), and who exists in heaven, viewed getting to heaven as worth an enormous value and, worth much more, than everything we own including all of our possessions in totality.

In heaven, it seems probable that time and space and even physical laws will be different. While not completely understandable, from Scripture, we can glean and understand certain aspects of heaven. We know that in heaven the Lord Jesus Christ "will transform our lowly bodies so that they will be like his glorious body" (Phil. 3:21). In heaven, "there will be no more night" and no need for "the light of a lamp or the light of the sun, for the Lord God will give them light" (Rev. 22:5). In heaven, "we will be with the Lord forever" (1 Thess. 4:13), and there will be "no more death or mourning or crying or pain" (Rev. 21:4). In heaven, we will dwell with God as it is written, "They will be his people, and God himself will be with them and be their God" (Rev. 21:3). In heaven, believers, along with many angels "numbering thousands upon thousands, and ten thousand times ten thousand," will be together worshiping God (Rev. 5:11), and everyone will shout out, "Worthy is the Lamb, who was slain, to receive power and wealth and wisdom and strength and honor and glory and praise!" (Rev. 5:12).

Chapter 12

Understanding the Future of the World

In addition to worrying about our individual futures, many of us worry about the end of the world. There are innumerable possible scenarios for this, such as nuclear or conventional world war, runaway disease and unstoppable infections, and natural disasters such as meteor strikes or earthquakes. Worrying about all of the things that could possibly go wrong is debilitating, but peace of mind arises from the knowledge and realization that God is supremely in control of events on this earth and the entire universe. God will certainly have as much oversight in the end of the world as he had in creating it in the first place. Two thousand years ago, when asked about the end of the age by his disciples, Jesus said,

> "You will be hearing of wars and rumors of wars. See that you are not frightened, for those things must take place, but that is not yet the end. For nation will rise against nation, and kingdom against kingdom, and in various places there will be famines and earthquakes. But all these things are merely the beginning of birth pangs" (Matt. 24:6–8, NASB).

Thus, living in this fallen world will always be challenging and full of trials and tribulations. However, it is very interesting that Jesus uses the term, *birth pains,* to describe these future horrific events. Birth pains are terrible pains but are unique as while they are agonizing, after a time, they go away, and then are succeeded by wonderful joy. What joy does God have planned in the future for mankind?

Studying Scripture can tell us a lot about the future. That is because Scripture in the Bible contains many prophecies, estimated to be "over one thousand predictive prophecies," but only "half of these already been literally fulfilled" (LaHaye and Hindson 2006). A detailed study about events, which will happen in the future, as related to the five hundred unfilled prophecies is beyond the scope of this book. Furthermore, prophecies about the future are generally difficult to interpret and understand as God's revelation, while containing many clues, sometimes does not seem to have clear meaning until the time is right to have their meanings revealed. Nevertheless, with a humble heart, this chapter provides a synopsis of future events, which are generally well understood and clear in Scripture. The future events, which will be described are the most important for Understanding Manna and include the following: the Rapture, the Great Tribulation, the Second Coming of Christ, the Millennial Kingdom, the White Throne Judgment, and the New Heaven and the New Earth.

The Rapture

The term, *rapture,* according to the Oxford Dictionary means "a feeling of intense pleasure or joy." While the word, "*rapture,*" is not directly found in the Bible, it is a useful concept to describe a future event for those who have accepted Christ as their savior. Clues about the rapture are described in the following passages, "For the coming of the Son of Man will be just like the days of Noah. For as in those days before the flood they were eating and drinking, marrying and giving in marriage, until the day that Noah entered the ark, and they did not understand until the flood came and took them all away; so will the coming of the Son of Man be. Then there will be two men in the field; one will be taken and one will be left. Two women will be grinding at the mill; one will be taken and one will be left" (Matt. 24:37–41, NASB). Additional details about who *will be taken* are described in the following passages, "For the Lord Himself will descend from heaven with a shout, with the voice of the archangel and with the trumpet of God, and the dead in Christ will rise first. Then we who are alive and remain will be caught up together with them in the clouds to meet the Lord in the air, and so we shall always be with the Lord" (1 Thess. 4:16–17, NASB).

From these passages, it can be understood that at some unannounced moment in the future, while people are going about their normal activities *such as eating and drinking, marrying, and giving in marriage,* Jesus will come and take out his body of true believers. Characteristics of the rapture are that it will occur suddenly, will come at an unexpected time, and may come at any time present or future (which is why we always need to be ready). Very interestingly, when the rapture occurs, it will come about in a time period *just like the days of Noah.* In the days of Noah, soon after Noah, his wife, his sons, and his sons' wives left the ground and entered the safety of the ark—the great flood came. All of the earth was then destroyed by the flood, and all of humanity was killed, other than those which were taken out by the ark. During the rapture, analogous to the time of Noah, the believers will be taken out for a specific reason as well. The purpose is to save them from experiencing another worldwide calamity, which will be the most terrifying time period unlike any the world has ever known, called the *Great Tribulation.* Those who are alive during this time and, are not taken out by the rapture of Christ, will have to go through the darkest days that humanity will ever experience.

The Great Tribulation

The Great Tribulation is a future event, which will occur during a time where there will be an "increase of wickedness" (Matt. 24:12) in the world and a great rebellion against God. It will be a time, analogous to that prior to the Great Flood, when the world needs to be cleansed and the people punished. The period of Tribulation will last a total of seven years and will be so terrible that Jesus said, "If those days had not been cut short, no one would survive, but for the sake of the elect those days will be shortened" (Matt. 24:22). It is during this time that the Antichrist, empowered by the devil, will rise to world prominence. Following this, the world will be systematically destroyed through successive judgments and "every living thing in the sea will die" (Rev. 16:3, NASB).

During a specific five-month time period, people will supernaturally be prevented from dying and "people will seek death but will not find it; they will long to die, but death will elude them" (Rev. 9:6). Everyone will be tormented with unimaginable fear as described in the following passage, "The kings of the earth and the great men and the commanders and the rich and the strong and every slave and free man hid themselves in the caves and among the rocks of the mountains; and they said to the mountains and to the rocks, 'Fall on us and hide us from the presence of Him who sits on the throne, and from the wrath of the Lamb; for the great day of their wrath has come, and who is able to stand?'" (Rev. 6:15–17, NASB). Ultimately, by the end of the tribulation period, mankind will be decimated and "two-thirds will be struck down and perish" (Zech. 13:8).

The period of Tribulation occurs, not only because God wants to punish humanity for its wickedness, but also so that as many people as possible will come to salvation during this time. The continuous series of judgments, involving plagues and calamities, that befall the earth and torment mankind are designed to bring repentance by breaking down individual pride, destroying the spirit of disobedience, and humbling the strong to the point of helplessness so that they may turn to God. Although believers in Christ are taken out prior to the Great Tribulation, God will nevertheless appoint many new witnesses during this time, including servants for God numbering "144,000 from all the tribes of Israel" (Rev. 7:3), two witnesses in Jerusalem—who cannot be killed until the appointed time and who will "prophesy for twelve hundred and sixty days, clothed in sackcloth" (Rev. 11:3, NASB), and flying angels who will "preach to those who live on the earth, and to every nation and tribe and tongue and people" (Rev. 14:6, NASB). During the tribulation, along with uncontrollable fear and unimaginable suffering, the overwhelming authority and power of the almighty God will be fully on display. Many will finally repent of their sins, but others will become so hardened against God that they will curse God and be irretrievably lost.

The Second Coming of Christ

Jesus first came on the earth as the Lamb who was slain and through his blood "purchased for God persons from every tribe and language and people and nation" (Rev. 5:9). However, the second coming of Jesus will be very different as his role as the Lamb has been fulfilled, and Jesus will come as the "Lion of the tribe of Judah" (Rev. 5:5). Jesus's return as a conquering king will be clearly apparent and all people will see "the Son of Man coming in clouds with great power and glory" (Mark 13:26, NASB), and "every eye will see Him, even those who pierced Him" (Rev. 1:7, NASB). It will be a spectacular sight as Jesus will be accompanied with a great multitude of the heavenly hosts with the total number being "myriads of myriads, and thousands of thousands" (Rev. 5:11, NASB).

The power of Jesus's return will be overwhelming and undeniable and "when the Lord Jesus is revealed from heaven in blazing fire with his powerful angels. He will punish those who do not know God and do not obey the gospel of our Lord Jesus" (2 Thess. 1:7–8). Also, during this time, "at the name of Jesus every knee will bow, of those who are in heaven and on earth and under the earth, and that every tongue will confess that Jesus Christ is Lord, to the glory of God the Father" (Phil. 2:10–11, NASB). The result of Christ's return will be an end to the Great Tribulation, resulting in the defeat of the enemies of God during the final battle of Armageddon. Christ as king, along with the "the armies which are in heaven," (Rev. 19:14, NASB) will also defeat the Antichrist and the devil. This future event is described in the following passages of Scripture,

"He seized the dragon, that ancient serpent,
who is the devil, or Satan, and bound him for a

thousand years. He threw him into the Abyss, and locked and sealed it over him, to keep him from deceiving the nations anymore until the thousand years were ended" (Rev. 20:2–3).

The Millennial Kingdom

After the enemies of God are destroyed, Jesus Christ will remain on the earth and will rule for a thousand years in what is called the Millennial Kingdom. This reign of Christ was prophesized by Zechariah over 2500 years ago, in the following passage, "It is He who will build the temple of the Lord, and He who will bear the honor and sit and rule on His throne. Thus, He will be a priest on His throne, and the counsel of peace will be between the two offices" (Zech. 6:13, NASB). Mankind, having a ruler who is both the king and the high priest, is almost beyond comprehension and will usher in a new age of unbelievable peace and harmony in the world with the establishment of perfect justice and uncorrupted order on the earth.

During this time period, the earth, which was mostly destroyed during the Great Tribulation, will be rebuilt towards its original pre-fallen condition, perhaps like the original Garden of Eden. The earth will be a much different place as "creation itself will be liberated from its bondage to decay" (Rom. 8:21). An example of how it will be is provided in the following passages,

> "The wolf will live with the lamb, the leopard will lie down with the goat, the calf and the lion and the yearling together; and a little child will lead them. The cow will feed with the bear, their young will lie down together, and the lion will eat straw like the ox. The infant will play near the cobra's den, and the young child will put its hand into the viper's nest. They will neither harm nor destroy on all my holy moun-

tain, for the earth will be filled with the knowledge of the LORD as the waters cover the sea"
(Isa. 11:6–9).

Additionally, during this time, there will be no more training
for war, preparation for war, or need for war as described in the following passages, "He may teach us concerning His ways And that we
may walk in His paths. For the law will go forth from Zion And the
word of the Lord from Jerusalem. And He will judge between the
nations, And will render decisions for many peoples; And they will
hammer their swords into plowshares and their spears into pruning
hooks. Nation will not lift up sword against nation, And never again
will they learn war" (Isa. 2:3–4, NASB).

At the beginning of the Millennial Kingdom, Satan was
thrown into the abyss, which will be shut and sealed so that he
will be unable to "deceive the nations any longer." However, after
the thousand years are completed, the devil "must be released for a
short time" (Rev. 20:3, NASB) as described in the following passages, "Satan will be released from his prison, and will come out
to deceive the nations which are in the four corners of the earth,
Gog and Magog, to gather them together for the war" (Rev. 20:7–8,
NASB). This release does not happen by accident but is part of
God's plan and appears to be done so that the people, born during
the Millennial Kingdom, will be able to exercise their free choice to
follow God or not.

While humanity has been under the direct authority of Jesus
Christ as ruler and judge, some of the people may have been restricted
from revealing their true sinful and rebellious nature. After being let
loose and roaming throughout the world, Satan will then deceive
many who are not true followers of Jesus, and will then gather all of
them for a final battle against God. However, while gathered against
them, God will send down fire from heaven, which will devour them,
and Satan and his followers will be defeated. Satan will be "thrown
into the lake of fire and brimstone, where the beast and the false
prophet are also; and they will be tormented day and night forever
and ever" (Rev. 20:10, NASB).

The White Throne Judgment

After Satan has been defeated for a second time and thrown into hell, there will be a final judgment of mankind, which is called the White Throne Judgment. The White Throne Judgment is described in the following passages from the Apostle John's vision,

> "Then I saw a great white throne and Him who sat upon it, from whose presence earth and heaven fled away, and no place was found for them. And I saw the dead, the great and the small, standing before the throne, and books were opened; and another book was opened, which is the book of life; and the dead were judged from the things, which were written in the books, according to their deeds. And the sea gave up the dead, which were in it, and death and Hades gave up the dead which were in them; and they were judged, every one of them according to their deeds. Then death and Hades were thrown into the lake of fire. This is the second death, the lake of fire. And if anyone's name was not found written in the book of life, he was thrown into the lake of fire" (Rev. 20: 11–15, NASB).

Jesus who has been granted the authority of "all judgment" (John 5:29, NASB) will proceed over the trial of every person, not previously saved, during the White Throne Judgment. Those that are saved will be the exception, as Jesus said, "whoever hears my word and believes him who sent me has eternal life and will not be judged" (John 5:24). Note that everyone, who has not had their sins forgiven, will be judged and will get a fair trial. A lifetime of evidence will be presented, as everything that you have done in your life has been recorded and "there is nothing covered up that will not be revealed, and hidden that will not be known. Accordingly, whatever you have said in the dark will be heard in the light, and what you have whispered in the inner rooms will be proclaimed upon the housetops" (Luke 12:2–3, NASB).

After their fair trial, those who are found guilty in their sins will not have their name written in the book of life. The guilty will then be *thrown into the lake of fire*, which is the eternal hell. Those whose sins are forgiven by the blood of Christ will have their name written in the book of life and will avoid this second eternal death and enter the kingdom of God in Heaven.

The New Heaven and the New Earth

After the White Throne Judgment, the entire universe, including the earth, will be utterly destroyed as described in the following passage of Scripture, "The heavens will pass away with a roar and the elements will be destroyed with intense heat, and the earth and its works will be burned up" (2 Pet. 3:10). This is a grave revelation. which should guide how we live. The things on earth that we often hold as precious are not permanent, but instead they are passing and temporary, as the earth is not our final destination or our true home. Our true home is with God in heaven and "according to His promise we are looking for new heavens and a new earth, in which righteousness dwell." (2 Pet. 3:13, NASB). In heaven, "no longer will there be any curse" (Rev. 22:3) like that of the cursed fallen condition of the earth.

After everything is completely destroyed including all matter, a new heaven and earth will be created. The description of this unimaginable event is described by the vision of the apostle, John, "Then I saw a new heaven and a new earth; for the first heaven and the first earth passed away, and there is no longer any sea. And I saw the holy city, new Jerusalem, coming down out of heaven from God, made ready as a bride adorned for her husband. And I heard a loud voice from the throne, saying,

> "Behold, the tabernacle of God is among men, and He will dwell among them, and they shall be His people, and God Himself will be among them, and He will wipe away every tear

from their eyes; and there will no longer be any death; there will no longer be any mourning, or crying, or pain; the first things have passed away" (Rev. 21:1–4, NASB).

The apostle, John, further tried to describe the glory of this new dwelling place with God based on materials that he was familiar with in his day, "The material of the wall was jasper; and the city was pure gold, like clear glass. The foundation stones of the city wall were adorned with every kind of precious stone. The first foundation stone was jasper; the second, sapphire; the third, chalcedony; the fourth, emerald; the fifth, sardonyx; the sixth, sardius; the seventh, chrysolite; the eighth, beryl; the ninth, topaz; the tenth, chrysoprase; the eleventh, jacinth; the twelfth, amethyst. And the twelve gates were twelve pearls; each one of the gates was a single pearl. And the street of the city was pure gold, like transparent glass" (Rev. 21: 18–21, NASB). Thus, the glory of heaven is beyond description and unimaginable. The Lord Jesus said to Apostle John after this incredible vision,

> "Behold, I am coming quickly, and My reward is with Me, to render to every man according to what he has done. I am the Alpha and the Omega, the first and the last, the beginning and the end" (Rev. 22:12–13, NASB).

Chapter 13

Understanding Man

Previously, it was described how God directed history in a purposeful manner, and in the last chapter, it was discussed how God will direct future colossal events so that all prophecy will be fulfilled. Perhaps, God's plan connecting events over thousands of years may seem overwhelming (because it is!), and this may make you seem small and insignificant (which you are not!). This leads us to one of the age-old questions, which have been pondered by great philosophers and teachers and the common man alike since the beginning of mankind, which is *what is the meaning of life?* The question invokes many myriad responses including, from some, that there is no meaning to life at all. Out of all of the possible responses, this is the most depressing one of all, as it is based on a world model that we, as humans, just evolved from apes, which ultimately evolved from simple life forms. Thus, this model depicts humans, as animals only, which have evolved over time (i.e., millions or billions of years) and chance (i.e., random selection or survival of the fittest) and thus are no different than the animals. From this religion, there would be no absolute moral principles, nor right or wrong. Without meaning, your life would be lived without purpose, and when you die that would be the absolute end. Perhaps, the only significant meaning to human existence would then be contribution to the gene pool of the net generation but no more. Personally, I can't imagine what a fearful and scary world model this is, and wonder, how terrifying it must be for those who are living in this lie!

In contrast, consider an entirely different representation of the world, the Christian viewpoint, which believes that God made the heavens and the earth, that God created and placed mankind into his creation, that God provided absolute laws which are unchanging, and that God is firmly in control of events in this world. Rather than feelings of fear and tribulation, this view is comforting through the realization that you, or someone else that may be corrupt is not in control, but God is in control. It also brings abundant peace, consistent with faith, as described in Scripture,

> "Do not be anxious about anything, but in every situation, by prayer and petition, with thanksgiving, present your requests to God. And the peace of God, which transcends all understanding, will guard your hearts and your minds in Christ Jesus" (Phil. 4:6–7).

Many others are searching for *the meaning of life* through the pursuit of fame, power, and riches or through venerating, almost to the point of worshiping, sport's teams, individual star players, Hollywood actors or actresses, the social elite, or the politically powerful. Thus, many also get trapped in this lie as well, as it is enticing and seductive, based on the belief that if they can only reach a certain goal or their chosen idol, then they would finally be happy. However, once reached or obtained, often a new challenge is needed and pursued, as the old one, was found to not satisfy for long. Consider the many tales of lottery winners, who, after the initial joy and euphoria, some few years later, testify that winning the lottery had ruined their lives. The often hidden reality is that many of these people, which we idolize or wish to become like, actually live unhappy, unfulfilled, and even miserable lives. This observation of the misery, often found in the rich, the famous, and powerful, is probably a great puzzle for many, and one which they cannot understand.

The truth is that worldly things cannot satisfy for long as only Godly/eternal things can fully satisfy our desires. Jesus taught about this and said, "Beware, and be on your guard against every form of greed; for not even when one has an abundance does his life consist of his possessions" (Luke 12:15, NASB). Jesus also taught this parable to his disciples, "The land of a rich man was very productive. And he began reasoning to himself, saying,

> 'What shall I do, since I have no place to store my crops?' Then he said, 'This is what I will do: I will tear down my barns and build larger ones, and there I will store all my grain and my goods. And I will say to my soul, 'Soul, you have many goods laid up for many years to come; take your ease, eat, drink and be merry. 'But God said to him, 'You fool! This very night your soul is required of you; and now who will own what you have prepared?' So is the man who stores up treasure for himself, and is not rich toward God" (Luke 12:17–21, NASB).

While there are many widely different opinions on *the meaning of life*, the true meaning can only be derived from our Creator. When a lump of clay is molded into an object by its creator, the clay cannot know the reasons for the decision for its unique creation. In an analogous way, we are created by the Creator, who is God, and thus cannot know the exact reasons for our creation, unless told to us by our Creator. God tells us, that he "created man in His own image, in the image of God He created him" (Gen. 1:27, NASB) and that we were made unique to all other living creatures in that God breathed the "breath of life" (Gen. 2:7) into Adam. As we are made in the image of our creator, it should be clear that God would have made us with a purpose. Why were we created then? God provided this answer to the prophet Isaiah and said that people are "created for my glory, whom I formed and made" (Isa. 43:7). King David, who loved the Lord, said, "I will praise you, Lord my God, with all my heart; I will glorify your name forever" (Ps. 86:12). The apostle, Paul, wrote that "whether you eat or drink or whatever you do, do it all for the glory of God" (1 Cor. 10:31).

From the previous passages of Scripture, it is clear we are made to bring glory to God, but the next question is, how is that related to *the meaning of life*? This topic was examined in great detail through the writings of King Solomon, whose kingdom was one of the most powerful and respected empires in the ancient world, and become a world power having accumulated "fourteen hundred chariots and twelve thousand horses" (2 Chron. 1:14). During his reign, the Lord gave Solomon "rest on every side" with "no adversary or disaster" (1 Kings 5:4) to challenge his rule, until near the end of his life.

As a newly crowned king, God asked Solomon what did he want, and Solomon answered, "A discerning heart to govern your people and to distinguish between right and wrong" (1 Kings 3:9). Because of this humble answer, God blessed Solomon with riches and peace, but above all. "God gave Solomon wisdom and very great insight, and a breadth of understanding as the sand on the seashore" (1 Kings 4:29). Solomon's wisdom was so great that "from all nations people came to listen to Solomon's wisdom, sent by all the kings of the world" (1 Kings 4:34).

While reigning as King of Israel for forty years, Solomon experienced all that the world had to offer (but not without sin). Solomon was recorded as one of the richest men who ever lived. Not including "revenues from merchants and traders and from all the Arabian kings and the governors," Solomon received annually "666 talents" (1 Kings 10:14) of gold, which is equivalent to over one billion dollars today. King Solomon was so rich that he "made silver and gold as common in Jerusalem as stones" (2 Chron. 1:15). Along with being unbelievably wealthy, Solomon experienced life to the fullest including the pursuit of earthly pleasures, and he "had seven hundred wives of royal birth and three hundred concubines" (1 Kings 11:3). Thus, Solomon was able to experience in this world all of what this life can offer and in many cases with great excess.

Near the end of his days, Solomon reflected in great wisdom what he found out during his "life under the sun" (Eccles. 2:17). He summed up mankind's purpose as the following, "Fear God and keep his commandments, for this is the duty of all mankind. For God will bring every deed into judgment, including every hidden thing, whether it is good or evil" (Eccles. 12:13–14). Why should we *fear God and keep his commandments?* Jesus said, "Do not fear those who kill the body but are unable to kill the soul; but rather fear Him who is able to destroy both soul and body in hell" (Matt. 10:28, NASB). Furthermore, Jesus said, "If you love me, keep my commands" (John 14:15).

In summary, based on what God, our Creator, has revealed to us, *the meaning of life* can be understood which is the following: *willingly fear God and choose to keep his commandments, as by doing so, this demonstrates love for your Creator, which will glorify your Creator, and fulfill the reason why you were created.*

Chapter 14

Understanding Manna

The last chapter was about *Understanding Man*, including the reasons for our creation by the Creator, and concludes with the meaning of life. Understanding Manna is about the application of this knowledge in our daily lives as this knowledge is important to determine the eternal destination after death. For our bodies, various kinds of food are needed for nourishment, or we would starve and not be able to live on this earth. In Scripture, bread often symbolizes that which is needed to sustain life, and Manna is a special type of bread, which came down from heaven. After leaving slavery in Egypt and before entering the Promised Land, the Israelites wandered in the desert for forty years. Even though their assembly was extremely large (perhaps two million total) and the landscape was barren, the Israelites did not die of starvation. Instead, the Israelites were provided with Manna to eat by God, which sustained them physically during their time of tribulation in the desert.

Manna has been referred to as the "grain of heaven" and "the bread of angels" (Pss. 78:24–25). How Manna appeared is described in the following passage, "When the dew settled on the camp at night, the Manna also came down" (Num. 11:9). The Israelites would then gather the Manna for their daily food. However, the usage of manna came with rules, the Israelites needed to collect just enough for their daily needs, and it could not be stored up as it would turn rotten and would be not edible. The exception was the day before the Sabbath (i.e., the day of rest), when they were to gather enough for two days so that they could rest on the Sabbath. Thus, their daily food would appear without the Israelites needing to work for it and was offered to them by God as a free gift or blessing.

In our lives today, we are not wandering in a desert, but in an analogous fashion, we are lost and are wandering in a fallen world. We are all searching for something, and it is not the *promised land* in the land of Israel. This is because God has "set eternity in the human heart" (Eccles. 3:11), and what our souls long for is the *Promised Land* in heaven. This is why it is important to understand the full meaning of Manna. Jesus said,

> "Truly, truly, I say to you, he who believes has eternal life. I am the bread of life. Your fathers ate the manna in the wilderness, and they died. This is the bread which comes down out of heaven, so that one may eat of it and not die. I am the living bread that came down out of heaven; if anyone eats of this bread, he will live forever; and the bread also which I will give for the life of the world is My flesh" (John 6:47–51, NASB).

Thus, Jesus is the Manna *who came down out of heaven.*

It is also important to *Understand Manna* in the following passages, "To the one who is victorious, I will give some of the hidden manna" (Rev. 2:17). What can we do to become *victorious?* Jesus said, "Truly, truly, I say to you, it is not Moses who has given you the bread out of heaven, but it is My Father who gives you the true bread out of heaven. For the bread of God is that which comes down out of heaven, and gives life to the world" (John 6:32–33, NASB). Thus, we can be victorious by accepting the *true bread out of heaven,* who is Jesus, and by accepting his sacrifice and death on the cross, then we can enter the kingdom of God and gain everlasting *life.* What is the *hidden manna? Hidden manna* refers to the condition of those who are perishing, whereby their ability to *understand manna* is hidden, preventing them from understanding that Jesus *gives life to the world.*

Bread, while very nourishing, does not sustain for long, as our bodies need to be replenished with more food daily. In the same way, daily devotion to God through prayer is what God desires from us, as we glorify God through this devotion and our personal relationship with Him. Jesus taught his disciples how to pray in what has been termed the *Lord's Prayer* in the following verses, "Our Father who is in heaven, Hallowed be Your name. Your kingdom come. Your will be done, On earth as it is in heaven. Give us this day our daily bread. And forgive us our debts, as we also have forgiven our debtors. And do not lead us into temptation, but deliver us from evil. (For Yours is the kingdom and the power and the glory forever. Amen)" (Matt. 6:9–13, NASB). Our *daily bread* in the *Lord's Prayer* is Jesus, and we should dine on this manna *daily* as we live our lives on this earth. While Manna came down from heaven to sustain physical life, Jesus, the *bread of life*, came from heaven to sustain us spiritually, and partaking of this bread will lead to everlasting life.

Chapter 15

Understanding the Good News

As discussed previously in chapter 5 (Understanding the Biblical History of the Universe), the history of the world has been divinely engineered so that key events throughout history point to the Savior/Messiah, who is Jesus. The most singular and remarkable event in all of history is Jesus dying on the cross, and the most important and significant information that God has ever provided to mankind is the gospel message. According to The American Heritage® New Dictionary of Cultural Literacy, the word gospel, when translated from the original Greek language, means "good news". The *good news* relates to the fact that Jesus died on the cross and paid the penalty for our sins.

For unbelievers, it must seem surprising that for Christians, Christ dying on the cross is celebrated as a holiday, even more so that it is referred to as *Good* Friday. If Jesus was just a man, his death at the relatively young age of about thirty-three, would signify the premature end to a promising ministry of good works and could certainly be considered a tragedy. However, Jesus is God, and Jesus said that "the reason my Father loves me is that I lay down my life —only to take it up again. No one takes it from me, but I lay it down of my own accord. I have authority to lay it down and authority to take it up again. This command I received from my Father" (John 10:17–18). Thus, no one killed Jesus (see also chapter 7—Understanding Who Killed Jesus), but Jesus willingly laid down his life. Moreover, Jesus did not just die on the cross because his beaten and broken body gave out. Scripture records that, at his death, Jesus "cried out again in a loud voice, he gave up his spirit." (Matt. 27:50). Thus, in strength and in victory, Jesus *gave up his spirit* and became "sin for us, so that in him we might become the righteousness of God" (2 Cor. 5:21).

Jesus's death on the cross is good news (actually fantastic and wonderful news!) because his sacrifice brought a pathway for salvation to all and the gospel is a message of salvation. The singular most seminal event in your lifetime, if it occurs, will be the moment when you make a decision to accept the gospel message and the gift of salvation. This moment can occur right now and *Understanding How to Be Saved (Right Now)* is described in the next chapter. If you reject the gospel message, I pray that you will have another chance to reconsider this decision in the future. However, I would gravely caution to not bet your eternity that you will get another chance as "no one knows when their hour will come" (Eccles. 9:12).

It is important to reiterate that the events surrounding Jesus's life, death, and resurrection have been described and predicted in prophecy since ancient times and, previously a number of examples, (see chapter 4—Understanding What Is Truth) have been provided from the book of Isaiah as these predictive prophecies, fulfilled in Christ, are testaments to the *truth*. In addition to these prophecies directly about Christ, ancient prophecies also reveal God's plan of salvation. Prophecies related to the gospel message were written by the prophet Zechariah, who lived over five hundred years before the time that Christ came onto this earth. Consider the following passages of Scripture from Zechariah,

"Then he showed me Joshua the high priest standing before the angel of the Lord, and Satan standing at his right side to accuse him. The Lord said to Satan, 'The Lord rebuke you, Satan! The Lord, who has chosen Jerusalem, rebuke you! Is not this man a burning stick snatched from the fire?'. Now Joshua was dressed in filthy clothes as he stood before the angel. The angel said to those who were standing before him, 'Take off

his filthy clothes.' Then he said to Joshua, 'See,
I have taken away your sin, and I will put fine
garments on you'" (Zech. 3:1–4).

These passages reveal the basic concepts of the gospel message,
including that sin is something *filthy* staining the body, the removal
of our *filthy clothes* represents a cleansing corresponding to our sins
taken away, and once this occurs, future destiny is changed as being
snatched from the fire, which is the fire of hell.

Additional revelation about the gospel message in ancient times
was again provided by Zechariah with inspired writing about God's
servant the Branch, "Listen, High Priest Joshua, you and your asso-
ciates seated before you, who are men symbolic of things to come:
I am going to bring my servant, the Branch. See, the stone I have
set in front of Joshua! There are seven eyes on that one stone, and I
will engrave an inscription on it, 'says the Lord Almighty', and I will
remove the sin of this land in a single day" (Zech. 3:8–9). Thus, it
was prophesized that sin would be removed for all *in a single day* by
the branch. This is remarkable revelation and one, which must have
astonished ancient scholars. How this would be accomplished was a
mystery and would not be revealed for another five hundred years.

Who is the *branch*? The *branch* was described by the prophet
Isaiah about two hundred years before Zechariah in the following
passages,

> "A shoot will come up from the stump of
> Jesse; from his roots a Branch will bear fruit. The
> Spirit of the Lord will rest on him—the Spirit
> of wisdom and of understanding, the Spirit of
> counsel and of might, the Spirit of the knowledge
> and fear of the Lord — and he will delight in the
> fear of the Lord. He will not judge by what he
> sees with his eyes, or decide by what he hears with
> his ears; but with righteousness he will judge the
> needy, with justice he will give decisions for the
> poor of the earth. He will strike the earth with

the rod of his mouth; with the breath of his lips
he will slay the wicked. Righteousness will be his
belt and faithfulness the sash around his waist"
(Isa. 11:1–5).

The meaning of these prophecies is now clear, and the branch
is referring to Jesus who would come over seven hundred years after
Isaiah from the lineage of *Jesse*, who was King David's father, from
the tribe of Judah. Jesus would be the one who would remove sin in
a single day, which we now know occurred with Jesus's death on the
cross.

How can the good news of the gospel be summarized then? It is
God's plan for salvation, which was predicted by Scripture in ancient
times, it occurred in history exactly as prophesized, and, from our
current perspective, is based on historical events which were purposely designed. It is also a simple message that all have the ability
to understand (you may not understand as explained in chapter 2—
Understanding Why this Book May Not Make Any Sense to You).
The gospel message can be simply summed up by the following 6
themes;

1) *We all have a sin problem.*
2) *Sin separates us from God.*
3) *Jesus is God and came into this world as a man.*
4) *Jesus as a man was tempted but lived a sinless life.*
5) *Jesus died for the forgiveness of all sins (i.e., paid the penalty
   for all sins).*
6) *Jesus rose from the dead (i.e., was resurrected).*

Additional details explaining these main themes of the gospel
are provided below;

1) *We all have a sin problem*
   • Since the fall of mankind in the Garden of Eden, God's
     perfect creation has been corrupted.

- We are born into sin and all fall short of God's laws and continue to sin our entire life.
- Personal realization that one has a sin problem is the first step toward salvation.

2) *Sin separates us from God*
   - While sins can be committed against anyone, all sins are also committed against God.
   - God is a holy being who cannot and will not tolerate sin in his presence.
   - Sin, which is not pardoned and removed, results in eternal separation from God (i.e., Hell).

3) *Jesus is God and came into this world as a man*
   - Jesus is God and part of the Trinity; i.e., God the Father, God the Son, and the Holy Spirit.
   - Jesus has always existed and created the heavens and the earth.
   - Over two thousand years ago, Jesus was born through his mother, Mary, and the Holy Spirit.

4) *Jesus as a man was tempted but lived a sinless life*
   - Jesus lived on this earth as a man and experienced all manners of temptation.
   - In spite of these temptations, Jesus resisted them, and lived a sinless life.
   - Jesus is our personal savior and understands what we are going through in this world.

5) *Jesus died for the forgiveness of all sins (i.e., paid the penalty for all sins)*
   - Jesus lived his life unblemished and was sacrificed like the perfect Passover lamb.
   - Jesus offered up his life as a living sacrifice and shed his blood for the redemption of sins.

- Jesus died on the cross for all individual sins past, present, and future and for all people.

6) *Jesus rose from the dead (i.e., was resurrected)*
    - After being falsely accused, Jesus was severely flogged, crucified on a cross, and died.
    - After being in a sealed tomb for three days, Jesus rose from the dead and was resurrected.
    - Jesus who created life also conquered death and will lead his people (i.e., those that accept his payment of their sins) into the Promised Land (i.e., heaven) to spend eternity with God.

Chapter 16

Understanding How to Be
Saved (Right Now)

No matter who you are or how you live your life, you cannot escape death. Youth or good health only represent false security, as death from accidents or disease can occur at any age. Proper diet, vitamins, and exercise will not save you, even if you worship your own body and try every moment to be in perfect shape. No matter how much or how little money you have accumulated, or how much fame or power you have achieved, this will not save you from death. Thus, death is the great equalizer for all, with presidents, prime ministers, and kings on equal footing with the rest of us. In fact, nothing can secure you from death, and God, who exists outside of time, already knows your final second, of your closing minute, of your last hour, on your departing day. Constant fear of death provides no relief either, and Jesus addressed this when he said, "Which of you by worrying can add a single hour to his life's span?" (Luke 12:25, NASB).

Death is not the end; however, as after you die, your body and soul will be separated and you will continue to exist. Death is only a transition as you will go from a living being with freewill and the ability to make choices, to a condition where your soul is separated from the body and you are sealed in your condition. If you have not repented of your sins and accepted Jesus Christ as your one and only personal Savior, then it will be too late to do so, and you will die in your sins. At that point, you will be like a weed in an otherwise beautiful and perfect garden, which Jesus Christ described in the following passages, "As the weeds are pulled up and burned in the fire, so it will be at the end of the age. The Son of Man will send out his angels, and they will weed out of his kingdom everything that causes sin and all who do evil. They will throw them into the blazing furnace, where there will be weeping and gnashing of teeth" (Matt. 13:40–43). Alternatively, if you have accepted Jesus Christ as your Savior before you die, then you will be like a beautiful flower bountifully nourished and carefully protected in the perfect garden, which is heaven.

If you are not currently saved, then the question (I pray that you are asking) is how do I get saved? The pathway to salvation is described by Jesus in the following passages,

> "I am the bread of life. Whoever comes to me will never go hungry, and whoever believes in me will never be thirsty. But as I told you, you have seen me and still you do not believe. All those the Father gives me will come to me, and whoever comes to me I will never drive away. For I have come down from heaven not to do my will but to do the will of him who sent me. And this is the will of him who sent me, that I shall lose none of all those he has given me, but raise them up at the last day. For my Father's will is that everyone who looks to the Son and believes in him shall have eternal life, and I will raise them up at the last day" (John 6:35–40).

Thus, God desires that none of those created in his image will be lost, and that salvation is achieved by *everyone who looks to the Son and believes in him.*

How specifically then are you saved? This is summed up in the following passage from Scripture, "If you declare with your mouth, 'Jesus is Lord,' and believe in your heart that God raised him from the dead, you will be saved. For it is with your heart that you believe and are justified, and it is with your mouth that you profess your faith and are saved" (Rom. 10:9–10). To *profess your faith* involves humbling yourself, and then admitting that you personally have a sin problem and need a Savior. This includes the realization that sin separates you from God, who is a holy and pure being. Without this acknowledgment, you cannot understand the need for the Savior who removes sin and cannot have true faith in God.

There are no magical or specific set of words that one needs to say in order to be saved and to get into heaven. Being saved comes from the heart and only God "knows the heart" (Acts 15:8). If you want a new heart, God says that "I will give you a new heart and put a new spirit within you; and I will remove the heart of stone from your flesh and give you a heart of flesh" (Ezek. 36:26). If you want *a new spirit within you*, an example prayer, which you can pray fervently in your heart and speak with your tongue to be saved, is the following:

Dear Lord Jesus,

I admit that I am a sinner and have a sin problem and deserve to face the consequences of my sins. Because of my sins, I am in need of you, Jesus, and your forgiveness. I believe that you, Jesus, are the Son of God who died on the cross, rose from death to life, and will be coming back again. With great thankfulness, I accept the gift of eternal life that you, Jesus, offer through your death and payment for my sins. I trust in you, Jesus, alone as the only way that my sins can be cleansed and removed, due to the spilling of your blood. I proclaim that you, Jesus are Lord. I invite you, Jesus as Lord and Savior into every part of my life and ask that you, Jesus, would fill me with your Holy Spirit.

Amen

If you have prayed this prayer honestly and with all of your heart, congratulations, you will be forever part of God's kingdom! Furthermore, you will not have to face the judgment for your own sins. Jesus, the perfect sacrificial lamb, will now pay the penalty for your sins and "Though your sins are as scarlet, They will be as white as snow; Though they are red like crimson, They will be like wool" (Isa. 1:18, NASB). Your sins will be removed so completely from you that Scripture records that the distance of the separation of you from your sins will be "as far as the east is from the west." (Ps. 103:12 NASB). Furthermore, with the acceptance of Jesus Christ as your one and only Savior, this will not go unnoticed in the heavenly realm. Your conversion, from death to life, will be celebrated by the multitudes as "there is joy in the presence of the angels of God over one sinner who repents" (Luke 15:10, NASB).

However, if you did not or could not say this prayer, or a similar one, with all of your heart, then you will not be saved and you will not experience eternal life. Scripture teaches us that we are "destined to die once (i.e., physical death), and after that to face judgment" (Heb. 9:27). After death, your soul will live on and then await judgment. During the final White Throne Judgment, the books will be opened up, every detail about your life will be revealed and examined, and you will be judged fairly. After being found guilty, you will have to face the wrath of God yourself, and then will be separated from him for eternity and thrown into hell, which is the "fiery lake of burning sulfur" (Rev. 19:20).

Chapter 17

Understanding Why You
Still May Not Believe

As detailed in the last chapter, accepting Jesus Christ as your personal Lord and Savior is the most important decision that you will ever make in your life. If you have not yet made this decision, you still have time, but no one can predict how much more time you have left. Moreover, you certainly aren't in the minority by rejecting God (remember the wide gate from chapter 10—the gate that leads to destruction?). Believing in God (until Jesus returns in great power and glory with the heavenly hosts) involves faith, and this is by God's design to allow us to exercise our free will to make our own choices.

It is important to note that in this fallen world, we all struggle, and many unfortunate things happen, and only some of these seem fair or even are fair. We can easily become damaged, by living in this world, from direct experiences such as hurtful responses, broken trusts, painful memories, and undeserved tragedies. All of which may create barriers to accepting Christ. While your own situation is unique, please realize whatever is holding you back, whatever you have done, and whatever has been done to you can be overcome and forgiven through Christ. In the following sections, eight common obstacles to accepting Christ are presented and discussed in detail.

You Do Not Yet Understand

One reason that you may have to reject Jesus Christ as your Savior is you do not understand Biblical Scripture and the pathway to salvation. The message of the Gospel (i.e., the good news of Jesus dying on the cross to pay for your sins) may seem foolish to you, and you don't comprehend why it makes sense to others.

To help your understanding, consider the case of someone who commits heinous crimes such as robbery by gunpoint or murder, and then gets caught with clear and damming evidence of the crimes, including multiple eyewitnesses. Even as guilty, this criminal deserves justice through a trial and by a fair judge. A judge (and jury) must consider the facts in the specific case in order that there be justice, and it doesn't really matter if the person charged is a good person or not. That is, whether or not, the criminal sent his mom a birthday card that year, volunteered with the boy scouts, cleaned his sidewalk off every time after it snowed, or has given money to a charity will not determine whether he is guilty or not of the crimes charged.

Consider now that this criminal is justly convicted in a court of law, sentenced to death, and is now on death row waiting to be executed. The only hope now is for the death sentence to be removed by a pardon from an executive in charge, which may be by the president of the United States or, in some states, by the governor. The convicted criminal is clearly in a very desperate situation since a pardon is a very rare event. Certainly, if you were the guilty person living precariously on death row, wouldn't you accept this pardon and accept it with great joy and celebration?

A similar scenario to the previous example, occurred in 1833, in the case of an individual named George Wilson, who several times robbed the US Mail and wounded several people during these robberies and was convicted for his crimes in a court of law with the sentence of death. While awaiting his execution on death row, President Andrew Jackson pardoned Wilson. But then a remarkable thing happened, Wilson refused to accept the pardon. As this was the first time that this had ever happened and no precedent had happened previously, the case whether Wilson's refusal of a pardon was possible and legal went all the way to the Supreme Court.

During the resulting Supreme Court case, *United States Vs. Wilson*, Chief Justice Marshall defined a pardon as "an act of grace, proceeding from the power entrusted with the execution of the laws, which exempts the individual, on whom it is bestowed, from the punishment the law inflicts for a crime he has committed" (Sidney 1978, 36–65). Furthermore, in the Supreme Court ruling, it was declared that "a pardon is a deed, to the validity of which delivery is essential, and delivery is not complete without acceptance. It may then be rejected by the person to whom it is tendered; and if it be rejected, we have discovered no power in a court to force it on him." (Sidney 1978, 36–65). Thus, Wilson's refusal of the pardon was deemed constitutional and legal, and afterward, he was hanged until his death for his crimes.

Analogous to the case of George Wilson, as explained throughout Understanding Manna, we are all in a desperate situation essentially being on death row. We may not be in legal trouble with man's laws, but each and every one of us has committed many sins, and thus we are in legal trouble with God's laws, which are supreme. These sins that we have committed "have made a separation" (Isa. 59:2, NASB) between us and the Holy God, and thus we are all condemned and awaiting judgment. We will be judged fairly for our crimes, and whether we did some good things or good works along the way, will not determine the final outcome, as we must pay for the crimes charged against us, which must be brought to justice. After being judged, the resulting verdict will be either being found guilty for our sins or, even though we are guilty, as all have sinned, we will be pardoned for our sins. The pardon comes in the form of Jesus Christ dying on the cross, paying the penalty for our sins, and through his sacrifice and his blood, our sins are forgiven. However, we must accept this pardon while we still have the ability to exercise our freewill before we die, or we will have to pay the penalty for our own sins, resulting in being thrown into hell.

You Do Not Believe in God

One stumbling block in accepting Jesus as Savior is that you may not believe that there is a God. With this belief there certainly are a lot of questions with missing answers. Perhaps the most fundamental question is, where did all the matter in the universe come from? Did it just appear from nothing or was it created? The Lord says, "I will question you, and you shall answer me. 'Where were you when I laid the earth's foundation? Tell me, if you understand" (Job38:3–4). Also, it seems that it takes a stubborn soul to deny the existence of God, "For since the creation of the world His invisible attributes, His eternal power and divine nature, have been clearly seen, being understood through what has been made, so that they are without excuse" (Rom. 1:20, NASB).

Through observing nature, including its incredible diversity and complexity, its magnificent beauty and splendor, and its organization and perfect order, one can come to the clear conclusion that it has been designed and created by a creator (an incredibly inventive one!) who is God. Those that saw the Great American Eclipse, especially if viewed within the band of totality, would almost universally agree, how amazing and awe-inspiring it was to experience. For me, it was an incredibly powerful witness, similar to that described in the following passage of Scripture; the "heavens declare the glory of God; the skies proclaim the work of his hands. Day after day they pour forth speech; night after night they reveal knowledge" (Ps. 19:1). The bottom-line is that nature screams creation and this creation by an intelligent being cannot be ignored and should not be denied.

Maybe you are asking, if there is a God, then why doesn't God come down and announce his existence to all (this will happen during the second coming of Christ)? To understand this, consider when Jesus was dying on the cross after being whipped, stripped naked, and crucified. Try to imagine the humiliation he faced from this public display at Golgotha, which would have been located in a prominent visible position, for all of the public to see, outside one of the main entrances to Jerusalem. Scripture records the degradation of Jesus in the following passages,

> "Those passing by were hurling abuse at Him, wagging their heads, and saying, 'Ha! You who are going to destroy the temple and rebuild it in three days, save Yourself, and come down from the cross!' In the same way the chief priests also, along with the scribes, were mocking Him among themselves and saying,' He saved others; He cannot save Himself. Let this Christ, the King of Israel, now come down from the cross, so that we may see and believe!" (Mark 15:29–32, NASB).

However, Jesus did not respond to all of the taunts and hung there in humiliation until his death.

This was a purposeful and willful decision to fulfill the plan of the Father that he would die on the cross for the sins of humanity. Thus, the reason that Jesus, as a man, did not come down from the cross over two thousand years ago is the same reason that Jesus, as God, does not come down from heaven immediately and announce his presence undeniably and in great power to the world. All future events, as part of God's plan for the universe, will occur similar to past events, and only allowed based on God's timetable alone.

Absolute undeniable evidence of God, if presented or shown in great power, would certainly affect our free will and the ability to make choices concerning our eternal destination, and is not part of God's plan until "the times of the Gentiles are fulfilled" (Luke 21:24, NASB). At the appointed time, all "will see the Son of Man coming in A cloud with power and great glory" (Luke 21:27, NASB) with the multitudes of the heavenly hosts. No one will be able to withstand the awesomeness and power of God when he returns and "at the name of Jesus every knee will bow, of those who are in heaven and on earth and under the earth, and that every tongue will confess that Jesus Christ is Lord, to the glory of God the Father" (Phil. 2:10–11, NASB). How much better would it be, if while you are still able to choose, you get on your knees right now (you will bow either way), acknowledge the existence of God (you will either way), and accept God's free gift of salvation in order to be forgiven of your sins?

You Believe in God but You Are Angry with Him

One barrier to accepting God's salvation is that while believing in God, you are angry with him. Perhaps you have been treated unfairly in this world, or have been severely wronged. Perhaps you have been undergoing trials and tribulations or even severe tragedy. Whatever the reason, you blame God for your many troubles, reject his help and his grace, and may even hate him. This is a very difficult condition to be in, my heart goes out for your sufferings, and I pray for forgiveness and healing.

It is difficult to know or understand why your sufferings have been so severe, and I certainly don't have the answers. Sometimes, the reason why this occurs is not revealed and cannot be known. For example, there was an incident recorded in Scripture whereby an ancient tower fell in the south part of Jerusalem and several people were killed. Jesus referred to this event and said, "Those eighteen who died when the tower in Siloam fell on them—do you think they were more guilty than all the others living in Jerusalem? I tell you, no!" (Luke 13:4–5). Thus, they were not punished by God for anything they had done or even for their sins, but were instead innocent victims of a tragic event. In other cases, the meaning of suffering is revealed, as in the following example, when Jesus and his disciples in Jerusalem, near the pool of Siloam, observed a man blind from birth. "His disciples asked Him, 'Rabbi, who sinned, this man or his parents, that he would be born blind?' Jesus answered, 'It was neither that this man sinned, nor his parents; but it was so that the works of God might be displayed in him" (John 9:1–3, NASB). Shortly after this, Jesus healed the blind man and restored his eyesight. Thus, in this case, the reason why this man was born blind and certainly suffered greatly for many years was so that *the works of God might be displayed in him.*

This miraculous healing made such a stir among his neighbors and others who knew him that this formerly blind man was investigated by the Pharisees, who were part of the highest religious council of the Jews. They questioned him once, brought his parents in and questioned them, and then summoned him in for more questioning. Since the Pharisees did not believe that Jesus was a prophet, after questioning and hearing his testimony, they "hurled insults at him" (John 9:28). The formerly blind man answered, "Here is an amazing thing, that you do not know where He is from, and yet He opened my eyes. We know that God does not hear sinners; but if anyone is God-fearing and does His will, He hears him. Since the beginning of time it has never been heard that anyone opened the eyes of a person born blind. If this man were not from God, He could do nothing" (John 9:30–33, NASB). Thus, this man's miraculous healing and personal testimony, even though rejected by the Pharisees, would provide a powerful witness to all of the people, especially those who had observed his condition for so many years.

Sometimes, God allows suffering to test and strengthen our faith. Consider Jeremiah who experienced great trials and tribulations in his life about 2600 years ago. Jeremiah was a prophet sent by God to declare to his fellow Jews that Jerusalem would be captured by "the army of the king of Babylon" (Jer. 38:3, NASB). Jeremiah's prophecies, that Jerusalem would fall and that everyone needed to surrender to the Babylonians, were not popular with King Zedekiah or the people living in Jerusalem. Jeremiah experienced severe rejection and wrote the following passages,

> "I have been deprived of peace; I have forgotten what prosperity is. So I say, 'My splendor is gone and all that I had hoped from the LORD.' I remember my affliction and my wandering, the bitterness and the gall. I well remember them, and my soul is downcast within me. Yet this I call to mind and therefore I have hope: Because of the LORD's great love we are not consumed, for his compassions never fail. They are new every morn-

ing; great is your faithfulness. I say to myself, 'The
Lord is my portion; therefore I will wait for him.'
The Lord is good to those whose hope is in him,
to the one who seeks him; it is good to wait quietly
for the salvation of the Lord" (Lam. 3:17–26).

Later, Jeremiah's prophecies became such as stench to the people
that the officers of the King said, "Jeremiah must be put to death!"
(Jer. 38:4). After a time, the uproar grew so bad that the king relented
to their demands and Jeremiah was placed into a deepwater well that
was dry. When lowered into the well, Jeremiah sank deep into the
mud, was unable to move, and was left to die. Jeremiah's situation
was dire, as there was no food, no water, no warmth, and no escape
from the well. However, Jeremiah while severely tested, remained
faithful to God. Knowing the *Lord's great love*, Jeremiah persevered
in his faith and was removed from the well and even survived the
capture and destruction of Jerusalem.

Another important perspective to consider is that your struggles
and tribulations might be allowed by God, to get your attention, to
break down your own pride, to bring you to your knees, and to move
you powerfully to get you to cry out to God for help. The Apostle
Paul wrote about this and said, "We boast in the hope of the glory
of God. Not only so, but we also glory in our sufferings, because we
know that suffering produces perseverance; perseverance, character;
and character, hope" (Rom. 5:2–4).

God desires that you will put your focus and hope on him and
his Kingdom. However, it is easy while living in this world to get
diverted on the quest of other things, such as the pursuit of money,
power, or fame. Jesus said,

"Do not store up for yourselves treasures on
earth, where moth and rust destroy, and where
thieves break in and steal. But store up for yourselves treasures in heaven, where neither moth
nor rust destroys, and where thieves do not break

in or steal; for where your treasure is, there your heart will be also" (Matt. 6:19–21, NASB).

No matter how difficult your trials and tribulations, don't reject the living God, who is the lover of your soul and your place of refuge. Instead, seek out, put your hope in, and place all of your trust in Jesus who is worthy to receive, "honor and glory and praise!" (Rev. 5:12).

You Do Not Believe that You Have a Sin Problem

If you do not believe that you are a sinner, this definitely is a large stumbling block to accepting Christ. Without admitting that you have a sin problem, you cannot understand the need for a Savior. Sin occurs when we break the Law of God, which includes the Ten Commandments and the Mosaic Law, which are moral, domestic, and ritual laws (see chapter 5—Understanding the Biblical History of the Universe). If you casually look at the Ten Commandments, which are moral laws, perhaps you may think that you have not broken any of these. Let's examine this belief by considering just three of these commandments in more detail.

The Sixth Commandment says, *you shall not murder.* With respect to this commandment, you may think you have not killed or murdered anyone. With respect to the laws of mankind, this may be correct; however, God's standard is much higher. Jesus said, "You have heard that it was said to the people long ago, 'You shall not murder, and anyone who murders will be subject to judgment. But I tell you that anyone who is angry with a brother or sister will be subject to judgment'" (Matt. 5:21–22). Have you ever been really upset or angry with someone?

Consider also, the Seventh Commandment, which states, *you shall not commit adultery.* Jesus said, "You have heard that it was said, 'You shall not commit adultery.' But I tell you that anyone who looks at a woman lustfully has already committed adultery with her in his heart" (Matt. 5:27–28). Have you ever looked upon (outside of marriage) a man or a woman lustfully?

Now consider just one more commandment, the Tenth Commandment, which states, *you shall not covet.* Coveting relates to envy/jealousy against something that another person rightfully owns. Over time, coveting can develop into a strong desire or lust. Scripture teaches that once "lust has conceived, it gives birth to sin; and when sin is accomplished, it brings forth death" (James 1:15, NASB). Have you ever coveted the possession of another?

With an honest assessment of our lives and actions, considering only these three Commandments, the vast overwhelming majority of us would admit that, yes we are indeed sinners. Through studying Scripture, it is absolutely clear that the entire totality of the Law is powerfully inescapable and a standard of perfection, where if we don't keep it perfectly, results in sin. Furthermore, Scripture teaches us that "all wrongdoing is sin" (1 John 5:17), and furthermore that anyone who "knows the good they ought to do and doesn't do it, it is sin for them" (James 4:17). Thus, it should be understood that God's law creates a standard, which cannot be met by anyone who has ever lived (with the exception of Jesus, who lived a sinless life). While the type and combinations of sins are different for each of us, based on individual strengths and weaknesses/susceptibilities, we all have a sin problem. In fact, "Scripture declares that the whole world is a prisoner of sin" (Gal. 3:22), and that "all have sinned and fall short of the glory of God" (Rom. 3:23, NASB).

The first step toward being saved is admitting your sin and that you have a sin problem, which is paramount because "Sin is death." (Rom. 6:23, NASB). The law was never meant to save us but condemns us, through clearly exposing our sins. Once you become aware of your sin, you may then realize how desperately you need a savior since your sin separates you from God, who is a holy and pure being. Quite frankly, if you do not believe that you have a sin problem, you are in rebellion to God. Scripture says that

> "if we say that we have no sin, we are deceiving ourselves and the truth is not in us. If we confess our sins, He is faithful and righteous to forgive us our sins and to cleanse us from

all unrighteousness. If we say that we have not sinned, we make Him a liar and His word is not in us" (1 John 1:8–10, NASB).

You Believe that You Are Already a Good Person

In this case, you believe that you are a good person, but perhaps not a perfect person. Deep down, you know that you have sinned, can and do admit that you are a sinner, and during the quiet and stillness of the night, you may even be able to feel your sin. Yet you somehow believe that in your present condition, you are good enough to go to heaven. The thought process is generally something like this—you have done some bad things but believe that you are not as bad as your neighbor, or that guy down the street, or the criminal that you have seen in handcuffs on the news. It is all about the relative scale, kind of like grading on a curve for a college exam where, for example, in a tough course, the top score while only a 70 percent is rewarded an "A." This line of thinking is also analogous to a vintage balance scale, whereby as long as the scale is tipped in your favor, with your good deeds/works more than offsetting the bad things that you have done, then you will be ok and will make it into heaven. However, is this viewpoint correct? Does God grade on a scale or look at your life as a balance sheet?

It is paramount to understand that God is a holy being and won't tolerate being in the presence of your sins, which "have made a separation between you and your God" (Isa. 59:2, NASB). Thus, to get into heaven and exist eternally with God requires that either we are perfect without the stain of sin or that we are cleansed before we enter. God's standard of perfection is difficult for us to understand as we are imperfect beings surrounded in our daily lives by imperfect beings. Thus, our normal perspective relates to much lower standards. For example, in baseball, if you can get a hit consistently four times out of ten (i.e., .400 or 40 percent) then you are a star worthy of the hall of fame. If you are quarterback in football, a 70 percent completion rate on your passes would be considered an exceptional day. On a test, often 90 percent will earn you the highest mark, which is an *A*. There is a 99.994 percent chance that during your lifetime, you will not be killed by lighting (National Safety Council, Odds of Dying 2016). However, the Biblical standard is not 40 percent, 70 percent, 90 percent, or 99.994 percent, it is perfection. If you live your life mostly sinless and even you don't sin 99.9999 percent of the time, this is still not good enough since you have to be sinless 100 percent of the time.

The problem with sin is that it completely stains your being. It is analogous to making bread where "a little yeast works through the whole batch of dough" (Gal. 5:9), and just like yeast in dough, sin permeates our entire being. Thus, it does not matter if there is more good than bad, since the bad contaminants the entire body. One sin will permanently and forever separate you from God (unless you are cleansed) as stated in the following passages in Scripture, "For whoever keeps the whole law and yet stumbles at just one point is guilty of breaking all of it" (James 2:10) and "Cursed is everyone who does not continue to do everything written in the Book of the Law" (Gal. 3:10).

Thus, Scripture teaches us, that unless we live perfect sinless lives, we cannot go to heaven. After talking to a rich young man about eternal life, Jesus said to his disciples, "'It is easier for a camel to go through the eye of a needle, than for a rich man to enter the kingdom of God.' When the disciples heard this, they were very astonished and said, 'Then who can be saved?' And looking at them Jesus said to them, 'With people this is impossible, but with God all things are possible'" (Matt. 19:24–26, NASB).

How does God make it possible? It is by grace through the sacrifice and cleansing blood of the unblemished Lamb, the Lord Jesus Christ. Like the psalmist, please cry out to the Lord,

> "Be gracious to me, O God, according to Your lovingkindness; According to the greatness of Your compassion blot out my transgressions. Wash me thoroughly from my iniquity And cleanse me from my sin. For I know my transgressions, And my sin is ever before me. Against

You, You only, I have sinned And done what is evil in Your sight'" (Pss. 51:1–4, NASB).

You Believe that You Are Not Good Enough

Believing that you are not good enough to be saved by God is the opposite case of the previous example. In this case, you probably know all too well that you have a sin problem and both, realize and admit, all of your wrongdoings. However, for some reason, you feel unworthy of God's salvation. This viewpoint is understandable to me because all of us are unworthy of salvation (which is why it is called grace). What we really deserve is not God's salvation but punishment for our sins. However, we do not have to face the punishment, which we deserve. Jesus, even though innocent and without sin, willingly died on the cross for our sins, and his death was purposeful and worthy. Furthermore, Jesus's death was worthwhile as God does not want anyone to perish but instead "jealously longs for the spirit he has caused to dwell in us" (James 4:5).

It is important to reemphasize that Jesus, when he died on the cross, paid in full the payment of sin for all people living in the past, all living in the present, and all those yet to be born. Can you imagine the price of this payment paid for the multitude of all of the sins created by the totality of all people that ever lived and will ever live? This would include every type and combination of vile, dreadful, revolting, abominable, and loathsome sins imaginable (and even those which are unimaginable and unthinkable by most of us). Thus, it can be assured that whatever you have done, your sins pale by comparison to the true evil that has been done by others in the history of the world. Never be misled on this point, as without doubt, you are worthy to be saved.

Consider what the Israelites experienced, just before the Exodus and removal from slavery in Egypt. The blood of the Passover lamb protected all the inhabitants of each house, when the blood was sprinkled on the doorposts, according to God's instruction. Scripture teaches us that the Israelites were numerous and there were "about six hundred thousand men" (Exod. 12:37, NASB), which certainly included tens of thousands of firstborn males. Consider that this group would have been made up with a wide range of people, both good and bad, including almost certainly idolaters, criminals, and sinners of all types. Nevertheless, they were all saved by the blood of the lamb.

If you still believe that you are not worthy to have your sins forgiven, you are probably facing enormous troubles, have done terrible things, or have fallen into cavernous temptations. It is astonishing and incredible to realize that Jesus as God can understand our challenges and temptations living in this fallen world. Jesus, as part of the Godhead, became a man and lived on this earth and experienced all manner of temptations. Scripture teaches us that Jesus was made "fully human in every way, in order that he might become a merciful and faithful high priest" and "because he himself suffered when he was tempted, he is able to help those who are being tempted." (Heb. 2:17–18).

As an example of Jesus's understanding and mercy, consider an event recorded when Jesus was at the temple courts in Jerusalem, "The scribes and the Pharisees brought a woman caught in adultery, and having set her in the center of the court, they said to Him, 'Teacher, this woman has been caught in adultery, in the very act. Now in the Law Moses commanded us to stone such women; what then do You say?" (John 8:3–5, NASB). Jesus could have condemned the woman (although the Law requires both the adulterer and the adulteress to be put to death), but instead, Jesus replied, "He who is without sin among you, let him be the first to throw a stone at her" (John 8:7, NASB). The teachers of the law and the Pharisees, who dedicated their entire lives obeying the law, then through personal conviction of their own sins "began to go out one by one" (John 8:9, NASB) until all had left. Afterward, Jesus did not condemn the woman but declared to her, "Go. From now on sin no more" (John 8:11, NASB).

Just like the woman who was caught in adultery and deserved death, we all deserve judgment and just punishment for our sins. However, this is not what God desires, he wants us to cry out "Abba! Father!" and through a "spirit of adoption," he wants us to become "children of God" in order to share in his eternal kingdom as "heirs of God and fellow heirs with Christ" (Rom. 8:15–17, NASB). In spite of all of our individual sins, once saved our sins are forgiven, and there is "no condemnation for those who are in Christ Jesus" (Rom. 8:1). The only unpardonable sin is the blasphemy of the Holy Spirit as "every kind of sin and slander can be forgiven, but blasphemy against the Spirit will not be forgiven" (Matt. 12:31). Blasphemy of the Holy Spirit involves a total and repetitive turning away from God. If you are reading this book, it is highly unlikely that this has occurred as you are yet seeking truth. If you keep seeking, "the truth will set you free" (John 8:32).

As you read this, you may be trapped in the pit of your sins, and it may not seem possible that God could ever forgive them. However, for God, who spoke the entire universe into existence, forgiving your individual sins (which have already been bought and paid for at a very high price), is not a challenge. Jesus said,

> "Come to me, all you who are weary and burdened, and I will give you rest. Take my yoke upon you and learn from me, for I am gentle and humble in heart, and you will find rest for your souls. For my yoke is easy and my burden is light" (Matt. 11:28–30).

Thus, the invitation from Jesus is for all to *come to* Him, providing *rest for your souls,* and even though he paid the price for all the sins of mankind (including yours), his *yoke is easy* and his *burden is light!*

You Believe that You Need Good Works

In this particular case, you realize you have a sin problem, you believe (correctly) that you are worthy to be saved, but somehow you feel that you need something extra. That is, you believe that Jesus partially (either to a greater or a lesser extent) paid for your sins, but you need to add to his sacrifice by performing additional good works or sacrifice some part of yourself in some way, to make the final payment for your sins. Note that this was already described in chapter

10 (the Way and the Truth and the Life) with the concept of "Jesus + *X*" where *X* represents a variety of *works*. It is vital to realize that this concept of + *X* is against the specific teachings of Scripture, and often manifested in different religious cults.

Let's examine when Jesus showed the way to paradise (i.e., heaven) to the thief on the cross. When he was crucified, Jesus was hanging on the cross with two criminals who were also crucified on his right and on his left.

> "One of the criminals who hung there hurled insults at him: 'Aren't you the Messiah? Save yourself and us!' But the other criminal rebuked him. 'Don't you fear God,' he said, 'since you are under the same sentence? We are punished justly, for we are getting what our deeds deserve. But this man has done nothing wrong. Then he said, 'Jesus, remember me when you come into your kingdom.' Jesus answered him, 'Truly I tell you, today you will be with me in paradise'" (Luke 23:39–43).

A short time later, Jesus gave up his spirit and died. As the Passover celebration was near, the guards hastened the death of the two criminals by breaking their legs, which caused them to suffocate while hanging on the cross. From these passages, it is clear that the repentant criminal died shortly after Jesus had told him, "*Today, you will be with me in paradise.*" During this short time, the repentant criminal was not taken down from the cross, nor was he baptized. He did not perform any good works, nor could he have performed any, since he was nailed to the cross, was very weak, and was just struggling to breathe and survive. Thus, clearly good works are not needed to go to heaven, otherwise the repentant thief would not have made it.

The concept of completion of works (i.e., Jesus not Jesus + *X*) was further demonstrated by Jesus with his last moments on the cross as recorded in Scripture; "Later, knowing that everything had now been finished, and so that Scripture would be fulfilled, Jesus said, 'I am thirsty.' A jar of wine vinegar was there, so they soaked a sponge in it, put the sponge on a stalk of the hyssop plant, and lifted it to Jesus's lips. When he had received the drink, Jesus said, 'It is finished.' With that, he bowed his head and gave up his spirit" (John 19:28–30). When Jesus said, "*It is finished*," he meant that the work of salvation was accomplished and no additional works are needed, no new revelations are required, and no additional help is necessary. Thus, the body of work leading to the forgiveness of sins and salvation is not partially complete; it was completed by the death of Jesus. It does not need finishing; *it is finished!*

It is paramount to understand that salvation is achieved through Jesus Christ and through Christ alone, and if you try to earn your salvation, you will be in bondage to sin. While in Capernaum along the shore of the Sea of Galilee, a crowd following Jesus asked him, "'What must we do to do the works God requires?' Jesus answered, 'The work of God is this: to believe in the one he has sent'" (John 6:28–29). Thus, salvation alone comes from believing in Jesus who finished all necessary works with his death on the cross, "For it is by grace you have been saved, through faith – and this not from yourselves, it is the gift of God—not by works, so that no one can boast" (Eph. 2:8).

You Don't Want to Be Like the Christians

Perhaps the reason that you cannot accept Jesus, as your personal Savior, is that you do not want to be like Jesus's followers who are the Christians. Quite frankly, it is hard to write this statement and this section is included only, with much sadness, because of the idea that it may be a stumbling block for some. Occasions exist when nonbelievers decide to watch Christians closely, either openly or in secret. They then wait and observe sometimes for a long time, until they see what they are looking for, which is when the Christian stumbles. Note that nonbelievers watching Christians is generally a positive sign, as it seems to indicate, that they are still seeking something outside of this world, they are yearning to find truth, and that their hearts are not yet fully hardened. However, once a particular nonbeliever observes that their selected Christian friend, Christian leader, or Christian-based group has messed up/sinned, they often immediately reject the Christian faith. They may even be so emboldened to further denigrate (whether privately or publicly) Jesus as a false God.

The question is then, why do Christians mess up/sin? First of all, it is important to realize that many who say that they are *Christians* are not and by this masquerade are harming the perception of God's kingdom. Jesus taught the following,

> "Not everyone who says to me, "Lord, Lord," will enter the kingdom of heaven, but only the one who does the will of my Father who is in heaven. Many will say to me on that day, "Lord, Lord, did we not prophesy in your name and in your name drive out demons and in your name perform many miracles?" Then I will tell them plainly, "I never knew you. Away from me, you evildoers!" (Matt. 7:21–23).

Thus, based directly on the words of Jesus, it is probable that a significant number of self-professed Christians, are not true Christians, and are not saved.

Unfortunately, which Christians are truly saved and have received the Holy Spirit, sometimes is difficult to know and ascertain since only God "knows the heart" (Acts 15:8). Jesus said with respect to false prophets, "By their fruit you will recognize them" (Matt. 7:16). Fruit is something easily understood by all. What fruit means with respect to Christians is found in the following passages, "No good tree bears bad fruit, nor does a bad tree bear good fruit. Each tree is recognized by its own fruit. People do not pick figs from thorn bushes, or grapes from briers. A good man brings good things out of the good stored up in his heart, and an evil man brings evil things out of the evil stored up in his heart. For the mouth speaks what the heart is full of" (Luke 6:43–45). A Christian life should bear evidence of good fruit and they should be, doing their best, to live a life honoring God.

Nevertheless, many of us that claim to be Christians, are indeed Christians, and are saved. The question then is, do Christians sin? The answer is yes since the Christian is still a human and has a body with a sinful nature, which is often in conflict with the spirit, "For the flesh desires what is contrary to the Spirit, and the Spirit what is contrary to the flesh" (Gal. 5:17). Once accepting Christ, some fraction of the new believer's sin problem is removed and often, after a relatively short time, significant life changes may be seen. Nevertheless, we, Christians, are a work in progress and are becoming more like Christ over time. However, this process occurs over a lifetime, and unfortunately, we will still stumble and sin along the way. Thus, the extremely high, often onerous, standard (even close to God's perfect standard in some cases) placed on the believer by the watching non-believer, is a standard that quite frankly cannot be met.

I have often thought that it would be great, if once a person accepted Christ, that he/she would be instantly gone and removed from this world. However, this is not God's plan as he works through his body of believers for his ministry and his glory, while they are alive on the earth. Each person is unique and serves a complementary role, as described in the following passages,

> "As the body is one and yet has many members, and all the members of the body, though they are many, are one body, so also is Christ. For by one Spirit we were all baptized into one body, whether Jews or Greeks, whether slaves or free, and we were all made to drink of one Spirit. For the body is not one member, but many." (1 Cor. 12:12–14, NASB).

Thus, God's kingdom on earth, is made up of flawed sinful believers, who somehow make up one body of believers; each individual with a special role, and with God given talents and abilities, that can be used for God's kingdom.

It is important to note that while a believer is still a sinner, the difference is that the believer is not a slave to sin, and when sin does occur, it is generally with an internal struggle as this sin grieves the Holy Spirit. Thus, when a believer commits a sin, it is often followed up with a repentant heart. The apostle Paul summed this up as the following, "For I have the desire to do what is good, but I cannot carry it out. For I do not do the good I want to do, but the evil I do not want to do—this I keep on doing. Now if I do what I do not want to do, it is no longer I who do it, but it is the sin living in me that does it" (Rom. 7:18–20). Thus, for the nonbeliever, it is important to not base your hope on anyone in this world, including the Christian who is yet a sinner. Instead, put your faith only in the living God, the Lord Jesus Christ, and "may the God of hope fill you with all joy and peace in believing, so that you will abound in hope by the power of the Holy Spirit" (Rom. 15:13, NASB).

Chapter 18

Understanding What to Do If You Still Do Not Believe

If any of the reasons provided in the previous chapter, or any others not covered, are preventing you from accepting Christ as your personal savior, it is certainly not about your ability to understand, as the gospel message is not complex. Perhaps you are too focused on the *wisdom of the world*. The Apostle Paul summed this up in the following passages,

> "For the word of the cross is foolishness to those who are perishing, but to us who are being saved it is the power of God. For it is written, 'I will destroy the wisdom of the wise, And the cleverness of the clever I will set aside.' Where is the wise man? Where is the scribe? Where is the debater of this age? Has not God made foolish the wisdom of the world? For since in the wisdom of God the world through its wisdom did not come to know God, God was well-pleased through the foolishness of the message preached to save those who believe" (1 Cor. 1:18–21, NASB).

If the Gospel message seems *foolish*, this may be a spiritual matter resulting from spiritual blindness as described in the following passage, "You will be ever hearing but never understanding; you will be ever seeing but never perceiving" (Matt. 13:14). How do you overcome spiritual blindness? This is a very difficult question indeed as everyone's situation is unique involving pride, complex circumstances, stumbling blocks, and accumulated damage from living in a fallen world. Nevertheless, consider the following three examples of gentiles (i.e., not Jewish) recorded in Scripture, where each individual overcame severe troubles and tribulations, and ultimately accepted God through *obedience, faith*, and *perseverance*.

Obedience

Jesus said. "If you love Me, you will keep My commandments" (John 14:15). Also, the apostle John says, "this is love, that we walk according to His commandments" (2 John 1:6).

How should you obey God? You should obey God like Naaman, who lived in Aram (i.e., modern day Syria) about 2,900 years ago. Naaman was a great commander, was valiant in battle, and was greatly respected by the people and also by his king. However, while unequaled in battle, Naaman had one weakness as he developed leprosy, a disease that could not be cured and would slowly destroy him. Additionally, once the outward signs of leprosy became apparent, this would make Naaman a social outcast and a person to be shunned. Naaman, in all his greatness, could not overcome this problem. When Naaman learned from a servant girl from Israel, that there was a true prophet of God, named Elisha who could heal him, he took action. Naaman gathered up great riches and "took with him ten talents of silver and six thousand shekels of gold and ten changes of clothes" (2 Kings 5:5, NASB) and left with a great entourage, which included "horses and chariots." (2 Kings 5:9, NASB).

After arriving at Elisha's house, Naaman, due to his great status, expected personal attention from the Prophet Elisha, but instead was presented with a messenger who said, "Go and wash in the Jordan seven times, and your flesh will be restored to you and you will be clean" (2 Kings 5:10, NASB). Naaman said, "'Are not Abanah and Pharpar, the rivers of Damascus, better than all the waters of Israel?

Could I not wash in them and be clean?' So he turned and went away in a rage" (2 Kings 5:12, NASB). It was only after some time that his rage died down and his pride subsided.

Naaman had no other options to cure his problem and then he finally decided to obey God, even though washing in any river was not a known cure for leprosy. Naaman, severely humbled, traveled to the Jordan River and "went down and dipped himself seven times in the Jordan, according to the word of the man of God; and his flesh was restored like the flesh of a little child and he was clean" (2 Kings 5:14, NASB). After being cleansed, "Naaman and all his attendants went back to the man of God. He stood before him and said, 'Now I know that there is no God in all the world except in Israel'" (2 Kings 5:15).

Faith

To be obedient involves faith, which is defined in Scripture as "confidence in what we hope for and assurance about what we do not see" (Heb. 11:1).

What type of faith do you need then? You need faith like that of the Widow of Zerapheth who lived in Sidon (i.e., modern day Lebanon) about 2,900 years ago. Being a widow without support, raising a young son, she was already destined to be in extremely hard times. However, due to the evilness of King Ahab, there was a punishment of drought brought onto the land, which would last several years. As a result of the drought, crops failed, and there was a very severe famine for everyone, and all of the limited resources of the Widow of Zerapheth were almost entirely used up.

It was at this time that God directed the prophet Elijah to go to Sidon and ask for food. Elijah obeyed, went to Zaraphath, and met the Widow and then asked for food. The Widow said, "As the Lord your God lives, I have no bread, only a handful of flour in the bowl and a little oil in the jar; and behold, I am gathering a few sticks that I may go in and prepare for me and my son, that we may eat it and die" (1 Kings 17:12, NASB). Thus, all of the poor Widow's resources were gone and no options remained. Elijah told her, "Do not fear; go, do as you have said, but make me a little bread cake from it first and bring it out to me, and afterward you may make one for yourself and for your son. For thus says the Lord God of Israel, 'The bowl of flour shall not be exhausted, nor shall the jar of oil be empty, until the day that the Lord sends rain on the face of the earth'" (1 Kings 17:13–14, NASB).

Although the Widow and her son were starving, she obeyed faithfully and first made a small cake of bread for the stranger, Elijah the Prophet. Her faith, which was turned into action, would have gone against her instinct and every teaching of the world. However, she was rewarded by God for her faith and obedience. Through the remainder of the famine, as she opened up the jar of flour and the jug of oil, it was always miraculously full and she and her son were saved.

Persistence

Jesus described being persistent in the following parable, "Suppose one of you has a friend, and goes to him at midnight and says to him, 'Friend, lend me three loaves; for a friend of mine has come to me from a journey, and I have nothing to set before him'; and from inside he answers and says, 'Do not bother me; the door has already been shut and my children and I are in bed; I cannot get up and give you anything.' I tell you, even though he will not get up and give him anything because he is his friend, yet because of his persistence he will get up and give him as much as he needs. 'So I say to you, ask, and it will be given to you; seek, and you will find; knock, and it will be opened to you. For everyone who asks, receives; and he who seeks, finds; and to him who knocks, it will be opened. Now suppose one of you fathers is asked by his son for a fish; he will not give him a snake instead of a fish, will he? Or *if* he is asked for an egg, he will not give him a scorpion, will he? If you then, being evil, know how to give good gifts to your children, how much more will *your* heavenly Father give the Holy Spirit to those who ask Him?'" (Luke 11:5–13, NASB).

How much persistence do you need then? You need persistence like that of a Canaanite woman, who lived in a region north of Israel (i.e., modern-day Lebanon) over two thousand years ago. Upon seeing Jesus, this Canaanite woman, cried out and said, "Lord, Son of David, have mercy on me! My daughter is demon-possessed and suffering terribly" (Matt. 15:22). In order to test her faith, Jesus answered and said,

> "I was sent only to the lost sheep of the house of Israel." But she came and began to bow down before Him, saying, "Lord, help me!" And He answered and said, "It is not good to take the children's bread and throw it to the dogs." But she said, "Yes, Lord; but even the dogs feed on the crumbs which fall from their masters' table." Then Jesus said to her, "O woman, your faith is great; it shall be done for you as you wish." And her daughter was healed at once." (Matt. 15:24–28, NASB).

The Canaanite women humbled herself and bowed down before Jesus. She could offer Jesus nothing but her brokenness. However, through her tenacious persistence and great faith, her request was answered by Jesus, and her daughter was healed.

As the examples show, there is no exact formula for you to overcome the spiritual blindness, which you may be experiencing. Obedience, faith, and perseverance are certainly important tools for breaking down, whatever barriers prevent you, from accepting God's gift of salvation. Please never give up searching for the truth and, realize this is a very serious business, as you do not know when your time on this earth will end. Take this matter very solemnly and "work out your salvation with fear and trembling" (Phil. 2:12, NASB).

Jesus said, "whoever comes to me I will never drive away" (John 6:37), so always remember that you have an advocate in Jesus. Jesus knows more about you than anyone and, in spite of this, loves you more than anyone, and most importantly is a lover of your soul and wants to receive you into his kingdom. Yet, as a created being, Jesus has given you the gift of free will and leaves this decision, related to where you will spend eternity, up to you. If you cannot yet accept Jesus Christ as your personal Savior, I pray that you will keep asking, keep seeking, and keep knocking in order to find Jesus who is "the way and the truth and the life" (John 14:6).

Bibliography

Archer, Gleason, A Survey of Old Testament Introduction, Moody Press, Chicago, Illinois, 1994.

Blackstone, William, Section 2 Commentaries On the Laws of England, Oxford, Clarendon Press, 1765-1769.

Blake, William, "Voices From Solitary: A Sentence Worse Than Death", Solitary Watch, March 11, 2013, http://solitarywatch.com/2013/03/11/voices-from-solitary-a-sentence-worse-than-death.

Buchanan, G. Sidney, "The Nature of a Pardon Under the United States Constitution", Ohio State Law Journal, vol. 39, no. 1, 1978, 36–65.

Church, Alfred John, Brodribb, William Jackson, and Bryant, Sara, Complete Works of Tacitus, Random House, Inc., New York, New York, 1942.

Collins, Francis, "Why This Scientist Believes in God", CNN, April 3, 2007, http://www.cnn.com/2007/US/04/03/collins.commentary/index.html?_s=PM:US.

Ecklund, Elaine Howard and Scheitle, Christopher, "Religious Communities, Science, Scientists, and Perceptions: A Comprehensive Survey", Annual Meeting For the American Association For the Advancement of Science, Chicago, Illinois, February 16, 2014.

Ferguson, Robert A., Law and Letters in American Culture, Harvard University Press, USA, 1984.

Herman, Christine, "2 Million U.S. Scientists Identify as Evangelical", Christianity Today, February 20, 2014, http://www.christianitytoday.com.

Howell, Elizabeth, "How Many Stars Are in the Milky Way?", Space.com, May 21, 2014, http://www.space.com/25959-how-many-stars-are-in-the-milky-way.html.

"Hubble Reveals Observable Universe Contains 10 Times More Galaxies Than Previously Thought", Hubblesite, STScI-2016-39, October 13, 2016, http://hubblesite.org/news_release/news/2016-39.

"Introduction to the Holocaust", United States Holocaust Memorial Museum, September 3, 2016, https://www.ushmm.org/wlc/en/article.php?ModuleId=10005143.

Jull, A. J. Timothy, Donahue, Douglas J., Broshi, Magen, and Tov, Emanuel, "Radiocarbon Dating of Scrolls and Linen Fragments From the Judean Desert", Radiocarbon, VOL. 37, NO. 1, 1995, P. 11–19.

LaHaye, Tim and Hindson, Ed, Exploring Bible Prophecy From Genesis to Revelation, Harvest House Publishers, Eugene, Oregon, 2006.

Lawler, Andrew, "Who Wrote the Dead Sea Scrolls?", Smithsonian Magazine, January 2010.

Leshner, Alan I., "Public Praises Science; Scientists Fault Public, Media", Pew Research Center, July 9, 2009, http://www.people-press.org/files/legacy-pdf/528.pdf.

Morris, Henry M., Men of Science Men of God, Master Books, El Cajon, California, 1990.

Shalev, Baruch A., 100 Years of Nobel Prizes, The Americas Group, Los Angeles, California, 2002.

Whiston, William, The Works of Josephus, Book 18, Chapter 5, Part 2, Hendrickson Publishers, Peabody, Massachusetts, 1996.

Wyzanski, Charles E., "Nuremberg: A Fair Trial? A Dangerous Precedent", The Atlantic, April 1946.

About the Author

Daniel James Branagan is PhD scientist focused on the development and commercialization of paradigm changing disruptive nanotechnology that will transform modern design and functionality, allowing engineers to do "far more with less," thus magnifying market impact and benefits to society as a whole. Dr. Branagan is also one who readily admits that his scientific talents are a gift from God. He is in the mold of the *scientists of old* (and millions today) who had (and have) an innate passionate belief in the living God, and who's beliefs exists in perfect harmony with science and the observable physical world. The Lord says, "Let not the wise boast of their wisdom or the strong boast of their strength or the rich boast of their riches, but let the one who boasts boast about this: that they have the understanding to know me" (Jer, 9:23–24). With no formal theological training, but with "testimony in his heart" (1 John 5:10) and through understanding gained from *knowing God*, Dr. Branagan wrote *Understanding Manna*, with the goals of "setting forth the truth plainly" (2 Corinthians 4:2), and to testify to the good news of God's salvation "so that you do not grieve like the rest of mankind, who have no hope" (1 Thess. 4:13).

Marge,

I pray that the Understanding from this book will bless your life and your ministry!

Darrell James Branagan

CPSIA information can be obtained
at www.ICGtesting.com
Printed in the USA
FFOW02n0411230718
47486295-50776FF

9 781642 584523